S15418   616.9   Hyde, Margaret O.
616.9   Hyde, Margaret O.
HYD
     AIDS: what does it
     mean to you?

     $12.95

DATE			

AIDS
Acquired Immune Deficiency Syndrome

Recent books by Margaret O. Hyde

Missing Children
Cancer in the Young: A Sense of Hope
Sexual Abuse: Let's Talk About It (revised edition)
Mind Drugs (fifth revised edition)
Cry Softly, The Story of Child Abuse (revised edition)
Know About Smoking

and many others

Books by Elizabeth H. Forsyth
with Margaret O. Hyde

Terrorism: A Special Kind of Violence
Suicide: The Hidden Epidemic
What Have You Been Eating?
Know Your Feelings

Coming From Walker 1987.
Horror, Fright and Panic

AIDS

WHAT DOES IT MEAN TO YOU?

**Margaret O. Hyde
and
Elizabeth H. Forsyth, M.D.**

**Walker and Company
New York**

First published in the United States of America
in 1987 by the Walker Publishing Company, Inc.

Published simultaneously in Canada by John Wiley & Sons,
Canada, Limited, Rexdale, Ontario.

Library of Congress Cataloging-in-Publication Data

Hyde, Margaret O. (Margaret Oldroyd), 1917–
    AIDS: what does it mean to you? Revised.

    Includes index.
    1. AIDS (Disease)—Juvenile literature.
I. Forsyth, Elizabeth Held. II. Title. [DNLM:
1. Acquired Immunodeficiency Syndrome—popular
works. WD 308 H994a]
RC607.A26H93   1987   616.97′92   87-2031
ISBN 0-8027-6699-4
ISBN 0-8027-6705-2 (lib. bdg.)
ISBN 0-8027-6747-8 (paperback)

Book Design by Teresa M. Carboni

Printed in the United States of America

10 9 8 7 6 5 4 3

Contents

Acknowledgments

The authors wish to thank the many health care workers, medical experts, educators, and AIDS patients who have contributed to the research for this book. Special thanks go to Ben Forsyth, M.D., Senior Vice President of the University of Vermont and Professor of Internal Medicine; to Alan C. Lusch, Chairperson, Department of Physical Education and Health, Abington Township Junior High School, Pennsylvania; and to Michael J. Callen for permission to use "A Personal Report."

Groups that supplied information include: Centers for Disease Control; U.S. Public Health Service; AIDS Action Council; American Association of Physicians for Human Rights; and the National Gay Task Force. Current information came from the Journal of the American Medical Association and other scientific journals.

AIDS
Acquired Immune Deficiency Syndrome

1

AIDS: What Does It Mean to You?

AIDS has been called the health threat of the century, the world's greatest public health problem, and the most misunderstood disease of all time.

Many people who talk about AIDS know very little about it. They may not even know that its full name is acquired immune deficiency syndrome. The A in AIDS stands for *acquired,* which means that it is not hereditary or introduced by medication. The I stands for *immune* and indicates that it is related to the body's system that fights disease. The D stands for *deficiency* and represents the lack of certain kinds of cells that are normally found in the body. The S stands for *syndrome,* which means a group of symptoms and signs of disordered function that signal the diagnosis. Although the full name may not mean much to you, it is likely that you have some ideas about AIDS. It is also very likely that you will continue to hear about AIDS for a long time, especially as it spreads more widely beyond the specific populations it first attacked. What does the headline DEADLY VIRUS HEADING TOWARD MAIN STREET mean to you?

Five years after the discovery of AIDS, new information alerted the public to the need for drastic steps in order to prevent a grim scenario for the future. Feelings of hope for bringing the epidemic under control were mixed with feelings of fear. Some fears were realistic, other fears were based on misinformation, on prejudice, and on the fact that much remains to be learned about this new and deadly disease.

Many people sympathized with the twenty-five telephone repairmen who walked off their jobs rather than work with a man who had AIDS. A brilliant psychiatric social worker asked if she might have picked up the virus that causes the AIDS when she swam in a pool with a colleague who later developed it. A homosexual who had been promiscuous felt that he would never develop AIDS because he lived in the country; he believed that AIDS was prevalent only in big cities. One man who had only an occasional homosexual experience did not consider himself at risk. All of these people were misinformed.

In November, 1986, a major newspaper carried an article by a responsible reporter expressing the viewpoint that predictions about the spread of AIDS were exaggerated. The problem of AIDS was far less serious he said, than many people were being led to believe. About the same time, Dr. Halfden Mahler, head of the World Health Organization, announced a global program to combat the AIDS disaster, which he described as a pandemic. Dr. Mahler admitted that he had not taken the disease seriously enough at first, but now he said he was "running scared" and could not imagine a greater health problem in this century.

Doubts, fears, apprehensions, and ignorance about AIDS continue to abound. Myths and superstitions die hard, especially when many questions remain unanswered. But even though many people cannot bring themselves to believe it, there is no evidence that AIDS is spread by casual contact. The hysteria associated with fears of acquiring AIDS from swimming pools, restaurants, social kissing, sneezes, bathrooms, and any other form of casual contact appears unfounded.

The struggle between hope and fear is quite understandable. AIDS threatens millions of sexually active men and women, and it reaches around the globe. AIDS raises social, legal, ethical, political, and financial as well as medical problems. AIDS may be a national catastrophe in the making. Not everyone is pessimistic, but, even in the best scenario, AIDS will have an increasingly large impact on the world of tomorrow. In spite of phenomenal progress, AIDS is still considered one of the most difficult challenges ever faced by modern medicine. There is no cure on the horizon, and widespread prevention by vaccine is years away. Reports of new AIDS viruses add to the problem.

The virus that is responsible for almost all cases of AIDS today has been labeled with several names—HTLV-III, LAV-1, ARV—but is now commonly referred to as HIV (human immunodeficiency virus). Newly discovered viruses are called SBL, LAV-2, and HTLV-IV, but only the first two are known to cause AIDS.

Although a diagnosis of AIDS is not an automatic and immediate death sentence, as many as 75 percent of those diagnosed as having full-blown AIDS die within three years. They suffer from many diseases, and although it was once thought that AIDS did not kill directly, new information indicates that the AIDS virus can kill by attacking the nervous system. Also, since the virus destroys the immune system, people with AIDS are vulnerable to cancer and a variety of lethal infections.

Not everyone who is exposed to the virus will develop full-blown AIDS, with the malignancies, infection, and brain damage that can accompany it. The great majority of people who are exposed to the virus appear not to be susceptible to it, or they develop such mild symptoms that they do not appear sick. Evidently some people are more resistant to the virus than others. Genetic factors may be involved. Some medical experts suspect a "cofactor" such as another virus or drug use. Recent laboratory studies indicate that a person's general health may be an important factor, and that immune systems that have been weakened by various diseases may be more vulnerable.

Some individuals develop ARC (AIDS-related complex), and while no one knows how many of them will develop full-blown AIDS, estimates range from 6 to 20 percent. The distinction between the two is blurred; it is unclear whether a person has AIDS or ARC. In both diseases, people lose weight, lack energy, and develop fevers and swollen lymph glands. By some definitions, people with ARC do not develop life-threatening illnesses, but many people who have been diagnosed as having ARC have died.

According to one definition, only people who have depressed immune systems together with one specific major illness tied to the syndrome have AIDS. Under other definitions, the total number of people who have AIDS would increase by 14 percent.

Actually, in the exact sense, there are no symptoms specific to AIDS, but similar symptoms of infection are common in people with AIDS because of their defective immune systems. In its most severe form, AIDS is a collapse of the body's ability to combat diseases that a healthy immune system fights without difficulty, and these diseases usually cause the death of the average person with full-blown AIDS within eighteen months after diagnosis.

The incubation period of AIDS ranges from a few months to at least five or six years. There may be no telltale signs during this period. As symptoms become apparent, people with AIDS may notice persistent swelling of lymph glands in the neck, underarm, or groin area, recurrent fever with night sweats, rapid weight loss, constant fatigue, diarrhea and diminished appetite, and/or white spots or unusual blemishes in the mouth. In the later stages, the immune system of a person with AIDS becomes severely weakened. At this point, diseases that are normally mild and harmless can be potentially fatal.

People with full-blown AIDS are subject to a host of illnesses, particularly Kaposi's sarcoma (a form of skin cancer) and *Pneumocystis carinii* pneumonia (a parasitic infection of the lungs). These are normally rare diseases in the United States, but they are common and often fatal in people with AIDS. When the AIDS virus invades the brain, as it does in many cases, dementia is commonplace.

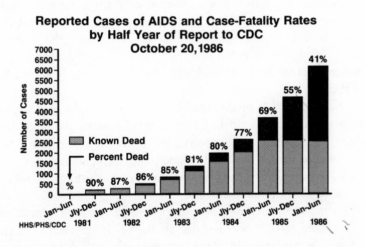

Experts predict that by 1991 there will be a tenfold increase in AIDS-related deaths. This prediction is based on careful studies, but many scientists believe that it is low, since AIDS is probably underreported by as much as 20 percent. By some estimates there are ten times as many cases of ARC, and no one knows how many of these people will develop AIDS or how many people they will infect. Suppose one adds these people to the one to three million already infected today. Dr. Robert Redfield of the Walter Reed Medical Center in Washington, D.C., suggests that the virus is likely to be present in the blood of from five to ten million Americans in 1991. Perhaps new drugs will be able to keep people reasonably healthy, or perhaps a vaccine will be available by that time. No one really knows, but the prediction of a tenfold increase is based on the number of people who are already infected.

People contract AIDS not because of their age, their sex, their race, or their job, but because of their behavior. High-risk behaviors are well known. Sexual contact, especially anal intercourse with an infected person, blood contact through injections or transfusions or by accident, transmission from mother to child account for almost all cases. Incomplete background information may be the reason for the relatively few cases that remain unexplained. Any individual with multiple sexual contacts, or whose partner has had multiple sexual contacts, is at risk for AIDS.

While AIDS is predominately a disease of males, both sexes now appear to be at risk. Comparatively few people have died from AIDS since its discovery, and even though AIDS is not easily spread, the threat of a much larger epidemic is real. For now, the only answer to bringing the epidemic under control is a massive educational campaign.

As mentioned earlier, people with AIDS are largely members of certain groups who indulge in high-risk behaviors. In the United States, roughly 70 percent of people with AIDS are male homosexuals or bisexuals (men who may be married, but indulge in homosexual as well as heterosexual activities). The disease is most frequently found among men who have had a large number of sexual partners.

Intravenous drug users who become infected by needles contaminated with infected blood make up the next largest group, at this writing about 25 percent nationwide, and this group includes both men and women. The percentage of incidence among these people is much higher in cities such as New York, where there are comparatively large numbers of drug abusers. There is growing concern about the spread of disease to the heterosexual population by drug abusers.

Some experts warn that teenagers and young adults in urban

areas are "ripe for a heterosexually spread epidemic of AIDS." Others warn that a balance must be found between panic and realistic fears. Many people are frightened for the wrong reasons. It is next to impossible for someone in your family, one of your friends, or you to get AIDS if the guidelines for prevention are followed. Knowing the facts about how AIDS is transmitted and avoiding dangerous behaviors are the keys to controlling this disease.

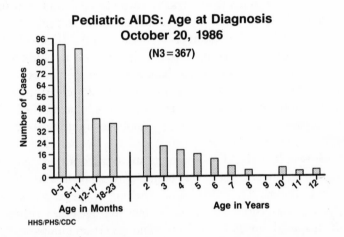

Pediatric AIDS: Age at Diagnosis
October 20, 1986
(N3 = 367)

HHS/PHS/CDC

Although the incidence of AIDS is still quite small among heterosexuals in the United States as compared with homosexuals and drug abusers, it has been increasing. By 1986, the number of cases traced to heterosexual contact in the United States had risen to 2 percent, a percentage point above that of the earliest years of the epidemic, and 80 percent of this group are women. Some cases of heterosexual transmission may be included among the unexplained cases. A total of about 7 percent of all cases may actually be the result of heterosexual transmission.

New evidence that the virus passes from women to men has

highlighted the risk of unprotected intercourse with someone who may be infected. The fact that prostitutes have been added to the list of unsafe blood donors, along with homosexuals and intravenous drug users, is indicative of the concern about the increase in heterosexual cases. Although the number of AIDS cases in this population will still be small, the Public Health Service predicts that the percentage will rise to 9 percent of the total cases.

Hemophiliacs and others who have received blood transfusions and blood products account for about 3 percent of the people with AIDS. The number of children with AIDS is small, but their plight is nonetheless tragic. In addition to those who were infected with transfusions, babies have been infected from their mothers. Exactly how it happens is not clear; it may happen before birth, during birth, or through breast-feeding. Some of these children are now of school age and the subject of great controversy.

Some people with AIDS belong to more than one risk group. For example, about 8 percent of homosexual men with AIDS are also drug abusers. The virus knows nothing of age, race, sexual preference, or ethnic background, but the activities through which it spreads are more common among certain groups.

Even though the percentage of people in each risk group varies somewhat from year to year, the relative proportion of cases in the highest risk groups has remained remarkably stable and is expected to continue to do so.

It is frightening to consider that an estimated one to three million people in the United States and ten million worldwide are now infected with the AIDS virus. It is more frightening to consider that these people can spread the disease even though they have no symptoms. Many of them will do so quite innocently. No wonder people are asking what they can do to protect themselves. No wonder they are asking, "Can AIDS be stopped?"

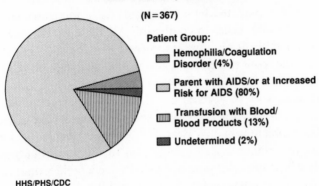

**Pediatric AIDS: Distribution by Patient Group
October 20, 1986**

(N = 367)

Patient Group:

Hemophilia/Coagulation Disorder (4%)

Parent with AIDS/or at Increased Risk for AIDS (80%)

Transfusion with Blood/ Blood Products (13%)

Undetermined (2%)

HHS/PHS/CDC

No one knows all the answers to all of the questions that are being asked, but two reports that appeared in the fall of 1986 played a major role in alerting the public to the necessity of immediate action. In these reports, health officials announced their growing concern about the threat of AIDS for the future. Both reports pointed out that increased educational efforts were needed immediately.

In 1986, the Surgeon General, C. Everett Koop, released a 36-page report that startled many educators and parents. He proposed teaching young children about AIDS, both in schools and at home, so that they would know about the risks of dangerous behaviors before they were tempted to participate in them.

Adolescents were among those targeted for a continuing campaign of awareness and of education in avoiding the spread of AIDS. For many teenagers, experimentation extends to sex and illicit drugs. AIDS has been called a young people's disease, so it is for this age group that education is especially important.

Another report, published at about the same time as the Surgeon General's, came from the prestigious Institute of Medicine of the National Academy of Sciences. This report, *Confronting AIDS: Directions for Public Health, Health Care, and Research*, was prepared by a committee with impressive credentials. Addressing issues in combating AIDS, in health care, and in public health, it was important in convincing many experts as well as the concerned public that the problem of AIDS is staggering.

For a number of years after AIDS was first recognized, the general public was only mildly concerned about it. Some people said the problem would go away. Others believed that the disease was a punishment from God, a form of divine retribution for people whose lifestyles were not socially acceptable to them. The policy of most religious leaders toward children and adults with AIDS is one of compassion and support, regardless of their sexual orientation or beliefs. Reverend Carl Flemister, executive director of the American Baptist Churches of Metropolitan New York, criticized fundamentalist preachers for encouraging the belief that people with AIDS are suffering for their sins. Rabbi Balfour Brickner of the Stephen Wise Free Synagogue has compared male homosexuals of today to Jews in the Middle Ages who were falsely accused and put to death by people who believed that they caused the plague by contaminating the wells of Europe. The unknown and unexplained have always caused irrational fears and social problems. Certainly AIDS has raised issues that go beyond the medical aspects.

As with many others serious diseases, people who are not directly involved tend to ignore the problem. They suffer from what has been called a "collective denial," continuing to view AIDS as a disease that affects "other" people. They are not interested in doing anything about it unless it involves someone they know or know about.

Rock Hudson's admission, in 1985, that his illness was a result of AIDS created new awareness and concern. Further increased awareness came with announcements that the disease is spreading into the heterosexual community. But along with this concern came panic and further isolation of people with AIDS and people in high-risk groups.

What AIDS means to you depends a great deal on your knowledge of the disease and how you choose to act. Compassion, as well as education, is one of the best weapons against AIDS.

2

Living with AIDS

Many people with AIDS have nowhere to go. Their relatives have disowned them. Their landlords have evicted them. They are not sick enough for hospital care, but are too sick to continue the search for other housing. Many hospitals, nursing homes, and temporary-care facilities refuse them because of the nature of the disease. Without the help of friends and support groups, they could be homeless. Even in the best of environments, facing death at an early age while suffering from one infection after another is brutal indeed. But, in spite of tremendous suffering, many people with AIDS have found the strength to reach out to others. They are helping in the battle against the myths that still exist about the disease that has attacked their immune systems and will bring on their death from the many other diseases to which they are prone.

Stewart was a person with AIDS whose landlord refused to renew his lease. This wasn't the first time this had happened; sometimes he felt as if he had been bounced from one place to another. Each time his condition was discovered, Stewart was asked to move on. At that time, he wasn't sick enough to be in the hospital. He could still care for himself, but he worried about what would happen when he needed nursing care. His money would soon be gone, but even if he were wealthy, the local nursing home would not accept him. Even an emergency shelter might refuse him. So he worried about where he would go when his lease ran out.

For a long time after Stewart knew that he had AIDS, he refused to accept any of the help that was available from groups such as the Gay Men's Health Center in his city. He had always been able to help himself. He was always proud of being in control of his life, but now he had to admit that he desperately needed help. That help came in response to his first call to the hotline at the Gay Men's Health Center.

Almost at once, Stewart was told that someone from the center would help him find a place to live. Stewart wished he had called the hotline sooner, especially when he learned that a volunteer would visit him within twenty-four hours of his call.

Bob was a volunteer, and he was asked to be a "buddy" to Stewart. Buddies are trained to provide personalized, nonprofessional assistance to persons with AIDS. They perform tasks ranging from friendly visits to help with household tasks. They do not provide medical care.

Many of Bob's friends had died from diseases associated with AIDS, so he was no stranger to their problems. He understood Stewart's fears and some of the diseases he had already encountered. When Bob visited Stewart the first time, he realized how much this young man needed to talk about the rejections he had experienced, as well as his problem of finding a place to live when his lease expired. For some reason, Stewart seemed most upset about the refusal of a bus driver to touch a transfer that he had offered him on his way home from the hospital several weeks before.

Bob listened as Stewart expressed his shock at being diagnosed as a person with AIDS. He had always been so proud of his health, and now he had no control over his failing body. Hearing that one has any life-threatening disease comes as a shock, and for a person to experience feelings of intense anger, confusion, and a sense of loss at such a time is not unusual.

Stewart and Bob discussed the guilt problem experienced by many men with AIDS when they are in the early stages of their illness. Bob assured Stewart that most newly diagnosed homosexuals with AIDS search their past for sins. They ask, "Why me? Is God punishing me?" Many experience a resurgence of anti-gay feelings even though they thought they were well adjusted to their homosexuality. Stewart was glad he had told his family that he was gay. He felt sorry for the homosexual men who hadn't told their parents and who now had AIDS. He had read of a case where a father told his son that the disease was a punishment for his sinfulness in choosing a lifestyle that shamed the family. Bob reminded Stewart that lifestyles do not cause disease, germs do, assuring him that he should not blame himself for his illness. Stewart was relieved to hear that others had felt as he had. He had not been alone, either, in his early denial of the need for medical care.

Stewart admitted that he felt depressed about his illness and that he had been made to feel like a leper. He avoided contact with other people so that they would not be able to hurt him further. However, this had made him feel totally isolated from the world. His work as a writer had been lonely, and the number of his friends was small. This made their visits especially important, but, one by one, the few friends he felt close to had dropped away. Stewart's roommate had left long before he was diagnosed as having AIDS, and Stewart had lost track of him. For a while, Stewart found comfort in going to church, but he stopped attending after he overheard a remark about people with AIDS getting what they deserved. Even though some of the church members might accept him, he did not feel really welcome.

Bob assured Stewart that many people were so ignorant of the ways in which AIDS is transmitted that they panicked at the very thought of coming near any person with the disease. He might encounter many such people, but he must concentrate on enjoying his life to the fullest.

Enjoying life sounded impossible at first. Stewart had been suffering from one cold after another. The colds had seemed endless; each one lasted an unusually long time. He then had developed the flu, and this seemed to take all his strength. Stewart had felt that he was growing more tired with each passing week, but he tried to attribute this to the fact that he had moved so many times in recent months. Then he had developed oral thrush, a thick white coating on the tongue and in the mouth, caused by the invasion of a fungus to which immune-deficient people are susceptible. There were night sweats and numerous aches and pains. Stewart's doctor suggested that he cut his work load, but Stewart wanted to work harder than ever. By writing longer hours, he could avoid thinking about his problems.

Each time Stewart heard a news brief about AIDS on the radio or when a television program on the subject began, he switched channels. He had learned that no cure was expected in the near future. Any vaccine that was developed for the general public would be too late for him. His doctor had warned him about spreading AIDS to sexual partners, and he had abstained from sex. Life had been grim indeed before Bob came to his apartment with much needed support.

Bob encouraged Stewart to attend a support group at the health center. Here he met eight other men in various stages of AIDS. At first he was horrified by the appearance of one man who had lesions from head to foot. Would this happen to him? Some of the men looked healthy, but all had, at one time or other, suffered from various infections known as opportunistic diseases (diseases that take the opportunity to attack because of suppressed immune systems). The doctor had explained this to him when he was suffering from oral thrush.

After his first visit, Stewart began to look forward to the meetings of the support group. Sometimes the members just drank coffee and spoke to each other on an individual basis. They talked mostly about doctors, treatments, and hospitals. They talked about ways to survive.

At one meeting of the support group, there was a deep and heavy discussion of feelings, and at others the conversation drifted here and there. One man was searching for a wheelchair, after being refused by a store that would not rent to people with AIDS. Another man complained about having to cross so many names from his address book, which seemed to Stewart a strange way of saying he had lost so many friends. The most exciting meeting, as far as Stewart was concerned, was the one in which he learned of a small apartment that would soon be available to him.

The support group became more than a place to go. Someone remarked that the group was somewhat like the foundation of a house that kept it from sinking. The members of the group all knew that they were dying, but they could joke and laugh. There was a special closeness among the people in the room. No one was superior; everyone was kind and considerate. Each one contributed something to help the others.

Stewart shared his information about a dentist who was willing to take on patients with AIDS. The dentist wore surgical gloves, something that was already becoming a trend for dentists and their technicians before the discovery of AIDS. For many members of the support group, it was hard to find a dentist after the announcement that the AIDS virus had been found in saliva, so they did not mind the long wait for an appointment.

As weeks went by, Stewart's condition worsened. He grew thinner and could barely manage to climb a flight of stairs.

Stewart had to lean on Bob for many household chores such as doing the laundry, cleaning, washing dishes, and shopping for food. Although he disliked losing the ability to care for himself, his acceptance that he had AIDS gave him a more peaceful outlook. He was no longer angry or frightened, and he continued to look forward to the evenings with the support group. He developed a sense of dignity as he resigned himself to the fact that he would probably die within the next year. A legal advisor from the clinic helped Stewart to draw up a will and to make the arrangements for his cremation. Bob promised to carry out his wishes, hoping all the time that a cure would be found and he would not need to use these instructions for many years to come. But Stewart continued to fail.

Soon Stewart's doctor told him it was time for him to go to the hospital for a long stay. This was a hard move, even though Stewart had been hospitalized many times before due to infections that his impaired immune system could not overcome without special medical help. The first time Stewart spent some time in the hospital, medical personnel were afraid to be near him. His food was left at the door, and he felt isolated from all human beings. Since then, guidelines for the care of people with AIDS had been published and attitudes had improved.

This time, the nurses who cared for Stewart and other AIDS patients treated them with compassion. The precautions seemed automatic, and Stewart knew they were necessary. Nurses wore gloves when handling blood specimens, blood-soiled items, body fluids, secretions, and excretions, as well as the surfaces exposed to them. Blood and other specimens were labeled prominently with the special warning BIOHAZARD, and they were double bagged. Needles used for injections or drawing blood specimens were reinserted in their original sheaths and promptly placed in puncture resistant containers for disposal. Extra care was taken in these and in many other ways to make certain that the staff or other patients were not contaminated.

One day, when he was drawing blood from Stewart's arm, a

young doctor accidentally stuck himself with a needle that tore his glove and caused bleeding. He left Stewart's bedside and rushed to wash his hands with disinfectant. Stewart appreciated the fact that the doctor continued to treat him well. The doctor expressed concern about the accident, and other staff members assured him that he was not alone. Since the incubation period for the AIDS virus is long, the young doctor's blood would be monitored regularly. It was unlikely that he would develop the disease, but he often wondered about the risk.

By the time of the accident, Stewart had already begun to waste away. Bob visited him often and filled his room with balloons and posters. There were times when Stewart did not feel like talking, so Bob just sat with him for a while. Before Stewart died, Bob made a promise that he would work toward increasing the number of shelters for persons with AIDS. Stewart died before he could move to the apartment that he found through the support group, but even in the last weeks of his life, he had continued to be concerned about others who needed places to live. He was especially interested in hospices, for he had hoped to die in such a place. Bob had investigated this new kind of care and thought it was an excellent idea. In hospices, terminally ill people can die with dignity as if in their own homes. Patients can eat when they feel like it, can get up in the morning and touch familiar things, and even though they are dying, they retain some control over their lives.

Bob knew that the problem of shelter for AIDS patients would continue. Many proposed shelters were rejected by frightened neighbors who pressured religious caretakers not to use buildings for AIDS patients. Many who were ready to leave hospitals had no place to go because public protests destroyed new programs. Community education is certainly needed in most cities, where the number of people with the most severe form of AIDS continues to increase.

Many hospitals were having difficulty in dealing with the care and treatment of AIDS patients. Their high rate of cancer and infections, unexpected complications, and poor response to therapy frightened even the most well-meaning caretakers. However, some hospitals met the challenge especially well. San Francisco General Hospital is a large county hospital, and their AIDS unit had been called an amazing success. Roughly half the city's AIDS patients are treated there in a unit that provides optimum care from both a medical and a psychological stand-point. In addition to inpatient services, the hospital encourages such outpatient services as counseling for newly diagnosed people, support groups, low-rent housing projects, and a twenty-four-hour hotline. It has been suggested as a model for communities where there are a large number of AIDS patients.

In September 1985, several Maryland nursing homes became the first in that state to offer shelter to persons with AIDS. The state of Maryland began negotiating with nursing homes after the highly publicized case of a patient who left Johns Hopkins in Baltimore when he no longer needed hospital care. Since he found no other place to go, he had lived alone in a motel until a retired couple who read of his plight took him into their home. A younger couple with children took care of him until he died. AIDS patient advocacy groups are extremely pleased that nursing homes are beginning to accept AIDS patients and that some hospices are available to them.

After Stewart's death, Bob spent much of his time working in communities where the climate of fear prevented the establishment of shelters for AIDS patients. He was not ready to form another relationship with someone who would most certainly die, but he looked back on his time with Stewart as one of the most rewarding experiences of his life.

3

Michael Callen: A Personal Report

On May 10, 1983, Michael Callen, a young musician, addressed the New York Congressional Delegation:

I am speaking to you this morning to personalize the tragedy of AIDS. I will attempt to do this, but since what brings us together is the fact that you are politicians, I will also try to explain how the political context surrounding AIDS inevitably becomes part of the experience of each AIDS patient.

Each person's experience with AIDS is different. I can only tell you my story.

I was diagnosed with AIDS in December 1981, although I believe I was immune depressed for over a year before.

I have been hospitalized twice since then and continue to have my health monitored by my physician and by a number of privately funded research projects.

Although I believe I will beat this disease, I am continually confronted by the media reports telling me that no one has recovered from this syndrome, and that my chances of living past 1984 are poor. Figures provided by the Centers for Disease Control indicate that 80 percent of those diagnosed when I was are now dead. My life has become totally controlled by AIDS and my fight to recover. I begin each day by checking my body for Kaposi's sarcoma lesions and other signs of serious health complications. I am subject to fevers and night sweats and an almost unendurable fatigue. I live with the fear that every cold or sore throat or skin rash might be a sign of something more serious.

At age twenty-eight, I wake up every morning to face the very real possibility of my own death.

I am a member of a support group for AIDS patients which meets once a week in the cramped office of the National Gay Task Force. In addition, in August of 1982, I formed a support group of gay men who have been diagnosed with AIDS. Because we have no community service center or other space in which to meet, the support group I formed meets in my living room.

Whenever I am asked by members of the media or by curious healthy people what we talk about in our groups, I am struck by the intractable gulf that exists between the sick and the well: What we talk about is survival.

We talk about how we're going to buy food and pay rent when our savings run out.

We talk about how we are going to earn enough money to live when some of us are too sick to work.

We talk about how it feels to get fired from our jobs because of unjustified fears of raging and lethal contagion—fears based on ignorance and unfounded speculation—fears which are being fanned by the Centers for Disease Control's endorsement of the view that we may be carrying and spreading a lethal, cancer-causing virus—fears that AIDS may be spread by casual, non-sexual contact. . . .

We talk about the pain we feel when our lovers leave us out of fear of AIDS.

We talk about the friends who have stopped calling.

We talk about what it feels like when our families refuse to visit us in the hospital because they are afraid of catching that—quote—"gay cancer"—unquote.

We talk about what it feels like to be kept away from our nieces and nephews and the children of our friends because our own brothers and sisters and friends are afraid we'll infect their children with some mysterious, new, killer virus.

We compare doctors and treatments and hospitals.

We share our sense of isolation—how it feels to watch doctors and nurses come and go wearing gowns, gloves, and masks.

We share our anger that there are doctors and health-care workers who refuse to treat AIDS patients.

We share our tremendous sense of frustration and desperation at being denied treatments such as plasmapheresis because many hospitals fear that our blood may "contaminate" the machines.

We share our fears about quarantine—the rumors that separate wards are being created to isolate us from other patients—rumors that certain hospital workers' unions have threatened to strike if forced to treat AIDS patients or wash their laundry—rumors that closed hospitals are being readied for the quarantine of AIDS patients and maybe even healthy members of at-risk groups.

We talk about our fears that the personal data we have volunteered to the CDC to help solve the mystery of AIDS may be used against us in the future. We are asked if we have had sex with animals. We are asked to detail sexual practices which are illegal in a number of states. We are asked to admit to the use of illegal drugs. The answers to these questions are stored in government computers. We are asked to trust that the confidentiality of this information is being safeguarded—only to find out that the CDC has already made available its list of AIDS patients to The New York Blood Center. We wonder who else has seen this information.

Mostly we talk about what it feels like to be treated like lepers who are treated as if we are morally, if not literally, contagious.

We try to share what hope there is and to help each other live our lives one day at a time.

What we talk about is survival.

AIDS patients suffer in two basic ways: We suffer from a life-threatening illness; and we suffer the stigma attached to being diagnosed with AIDS.

The end to both aspects of this suffering depends on finding the cause(s) and cure(s) for AIDS. And that can only happen if research money is released in amounts proportional to the seriousness of this health emergency. In order to confront and challenge the ignorance and insensitivity which we, as AIDS patients, must face on a daily basis, we need answers to the pressing questions of cause, cure, and contagion.

The political context in which AIDS is occurring cannot be ignored. AIDS is affecting groups which remain disenfranchised segments of American society: homosexual men, heroin abusers, Haitian entrants and hemophiliacs. This so-called 4-H club has been joined by prisoners (most of whom are either Hispanic, IV drug abusers, or both); female prostitutes; and the children of high-risk groups who are also victims of poverty.

Despite the fact that in the four years since AIDS was first recognized, AIDS has killed more people than swine flu, toxic shock syndrome, Legionnaires' disease and the Tylenol incident combined, the response of the federal government to AIDS—the worst epidemic since polio—has been to ignore it and hope it just goes away. If such a deadly disease were affecting more privileged members of American society, there can be no doubt that the government's response would have been immediate and matched to the severity of the emergency.

As a gay man, I could never decide whether I should be pleased with how far the gay rights movement has come since 1969 or whether I should be disgusted and angry at how far we have to go.

The government's non-response to AIDS crisis has answered this question for me.

Whatever you and your colleagues do or don't do, whatever sums are or are not allocated, whatever the future holds in store for me and the hundreds of other men, women and children whose lives will be irrevocably changed—perhaps tragically ended—by this epidemic, the

23

fact that the Congress of the United States did so little for so long will remain a sad and telling commentary on this country and this time.

I do not envy you your role in this matter any more than you must envy mine. 1983 is a very bad year to be an elected official, just as it is a very bad year to be a gay man, a Haitian entrant, or a child living in poverty. And surely when you first dreamed of holding public office you did not, in the furthest reaches of your imagination, foresee that your duties would include having breakfast on a Monday morning with a homosexual facing a life-threatening illness. You can be sure that ten—five—or even one year ago, I could not have imagined the possibility that I, too, would be up here begging my elected representatives to help me save my life. But there you are. Here I am. And that is exactly what I am doing.

Thank you.

Michael Callen

On October 2, 1986, Michael Callen Spoke to the Annual Meeting of the American Public Health Association. Here are selected remarks from his speech:

There are a handful of us, estimated variously from 10% to 18%, that happen to be quite alive more than three years after our diagnosis and who intend to be alive for many more years. The unthinking notion that everyone dies from AIDS denies both the reality of—but more importantly, the possibility of—our survival.

I have met a great many others with AIDS. It is possible to identify two general types of responses. For some, AIDS is entirely about dying. For others, AIDS is a challenge to begin living.

I don't want to create the impression that all you have to do to survive AIDS is have the right attitude. But I have found time and time again that those of us who give up—who say to themselves "death from AIDS is inevitable, so why fight?"—seem to go very quickly. And the quality of their last days is often clouded over by that bone-chilling gray fog of despair and hopelessness.

In contrast, those who are fighters and say, "I'm not going to let AIDS control my life!" seem to hang around a lot longer. In addition, the quality of their lives often takes on a glow—a sense of purpose—that in many cases was previously lacking.

I myself have chosen to fight AIDS tooth and nail. After an initial rather serious depression, I rallied enough to say that whatever time I had left, I was going to make the most of it. My strategy was to get on with the business of living and deal with each obstacle—each illness—as it presented itself. And my life since my diagnosis has taken on that sense of extraordinary vitality, that immense feeling of the precious-ness of each moment, that others living during wartime have often described.

Again, I don't wish to create the impression that I am glad I have AIDS. But I'm forced to admit that if I survive—as it now appears I may—it will have been the best thing that ever happened to me. I am more the person I always wanted to be now—in a word, happier—than at the time prior to my diagnosis.

And I'm certainly not alone in my perception that hope is necessary to live with AIDS on a daily basis. I am but one of many founders of a unique movement—the People with AIDS self-empowerment move-ment. I can't be more eloquent than the founding statement of the National Association of People with AIDS.

"We are People with AIDS and People with AIDS-related complex (ARC) who can speak for ourselves to advocate for our own causes and concerns. We are your sons and daughters, your brothers and sisters, your family, friends, and lovers. As people now living with AIDS and ARC, we have a unique and essential contribution to make to the dialogue surrounding AIDS and we will actively participate with full and equal credibility to help shape the percep-tion and reality surrounding this disease.

"We do not see ourselves as victims. We will not be victimized. We have the right to be treated with respect, dignity, compassion and understanding. We have the right to lead fulfilling, productive lives—to live and die with dignity and compassion.

"Our purpose is to promote self-empowerment of persons with AIDS and ARC by:
- *Enhancing understanding through education and support*
- *Becoming equal partners with our health-care providers and service organizations*
- *Helping develop and implement the necessary services and programs that will enhance the quality of our daily lives; and*
- *Continuing to have control over and direction of our lives."*

Michael Callen is president of the People with Aids Coalition, in New York City. He joins volunteers and celebrities in fund-raising efforts.

4

Avoiding AIDS

Since AIDS viruses have been found in the saliva of some people with AIDS, can I get AIDS from kissing someone who is infected? How can I avoid exposure to this devastating and potentially fatal illness? These questions are more easily answered today than they were several years ago, although questions about how AIDS is spread remain. Most people now feel more comfortable about social contacts with a person who has AIDS than they did in the summer of 1985 when the so-called "plague mentality" developed.

People wanted to behave in a sensible and cautious way regarding this disease, considering the fact that medical doctors still had some questions about how it was transmitted. The general public asked questions that were numerous and varied. Some of their questions appeared foolish to anyone who had some knowledge of AIDS, but other questions were based on past experiences of people who remembered warnings issued at the time of other epidemics. Some questions resulted from the disagreement among doctors who had varying degrees of knowledge about the disease and its transmission, and different ideas about the amount of caution that was needed.

Tom was afraid to visit his cousin, Max, after he heard that he had full-blown AIDS, but that was last year. Now he goes to see him in the hospital and feels very comfortable sitting next to his bed for a while and shaking hands with him when he leaves. He feels upset when he hears of some of the things that happened to Max when he was first hospitalized for diseases associated with AIDS even before he developed the most severe form of the disease. Max told Tom that his experiences were different each time, but today was the biggest surprise he had had in a long time. His meals were served on REAL dishes. Tom had never thought much about the kind of dishes he used, but during Max's past hospitalizations, meals had been served on paper plates so they could be destroyed after he used them. Max said that other things at the hospital had changed, too. There was no sign on his door that said AIDS—DO NOT ENTER. Although there were still caution notices about the handling of blood, the whole atmosphere was more relaxed than during his earlier hospital visits. Then, his breakfast grew cold on the floor outside his room where it had been left. When he rang for the nurse, one arrived in surgical gown, gloves, and a mask. She stayed as far away from him as possible, doing only what had to be done and leaving quickly without conversation. He not only felt sick, he felt shunned and very frightened. Now, the nurses and doctors seemed more comfortable when they examined him and tended to his needs. Even though his condition had worsened, he no longer felt like an alien. He began to feel like a human being again. Tom felt better about himself, too. He no longer cringed at the idea of visiting Max and shaking his hand. In fact, he felt good about supporting his cousin.

What about the families of people with AIDS? How safe are they?

Boarding school living is similar in many ways to living in a family. A study made in a Belgian boarding school with 25 children who had contracted AIDS from blood transfusions gives comfort to families of people with AIDS. These children slept in the same dormitories, ate in the same dining area, and went to class with the children who were not infected. The children with AIDS lived with the others for a period of one to three years without any spread to their healthy classmates.

A study of families, conducted at Montefiore Medical Center in the Bronx, included children, siblings, parents, and others who had lived with a person with AIDS over periods ranging from three months to four years. Most of the families were poor and lived in crowded conditions. Many members shared household facilities, some of which were soiled with bodily secretions from the patients. Combs, toothbrushes, clothing, drinking glasses, hugs and kisses were shared, but there were no sexual relations between household members and the patients. Of the 149 people who lived with 59 AIDS patients, only one child showed evidence of infection. Since her mother was an infected drug abuser, it is believed that the child was infected at birth.

Not everyone agrees that these studies prove conclusively that AIDS is not spread by casual contact, and studies will continue to be made with larger numbers of individuals. One case has been reported in which a mother was infected after caring for her child, but this was a very unusual case. The child was born with an intestinal abnormality and received blood transfusions from at least 26 donors. He developed AIDS from transfused blood and continued to need specialized care. His mother frequently handled his blood, his wastes, and his feeding tubes. She did not always wear gloves or wash her hands immediately after contact, perhaps because she was under great strain in caring for her very sick child. In the first five years after the discovery of AIDS, hers was the only reported case of nonsexual transmission in a family situation where intravenous drugs were not involved.

Avoiding AIDS is less difficult, even in close circumstances, when one is aware that a person has AIDS. However, as mentioned earlier, there are more than a million people in the United States who have no symptoms and who can spread the disease. This number is expected to increase through the years. If you do not know who they are, what can you do to avoid AIDS?

The answer to this question is well established. Since AIDS is spread through sexual contact and blood or blood products, you can avoid certain dangerous behaviors. "Anyone who is sexually active, visits prostitutes, or has casual sex needs to be concerned," says Margaret A. Fischl, director of the AIDS program at the University of Miami. Other health experts warn that any sexually active individual is at risk, but the risk is greater in some cases than in others. One risk factor is multiple sexual partners, but the disease can be spread by contact with a single infected individual.

Certain homosexual activities are the most common method of transmission of AIDS. Homosexual communities have done much to educate their members about safe sex, and in some areas, this appears to have helped in the battle against the spread of this dread disease. But disagreement about what constitutes "safe sex" still exists, with many health experts arguing in favor of the use of the words "safer sex." They feel that there are so many unknowns that it would be irresponsible to certify any particular activity, other than abstinence, as absolutely safe.

Today, it is known that the virus can travel from male to male, from male to female, and from female to male. Although the exact mode of transmission through sexual activity is still somewhat controversial, it is believed that the AIDS virus is a passenger in semen, and that it reaches the mucous membranes inside the vagina or rectum during intercourse. This tissue is much thinner than the skin on the outside of the body, making it more susceptible to tearing. When microscopic tears occur during vaginal or anal intercourse, the virus may find its way into the body through small blood vessels and establish itself in the genetic material of cells. An infected person remains infected for a lifetime, even though he or she may not develop full-blown AIDS within the first few years after infection takes place. No one knows whether or not infected people will develop the disease eventually.

In addition to being carried into the body by semen, the AIDS virus may be transmitted from women to men through blood or other secretions during intercourse. Although the incidence of transmission from female to male is much less frequent in the United States than male to male and male to female, such transmission appears to be common in some other countries. In spite of the tremendous amount that scientists have learned about AIDS, they do not yet know all the answers about how AIDS is transmitted.

It is known that AIDS is strongly associated with a highly active sex life, but it is not impossible for it to be transmitted through a single contact. People who abstain from sexual intercourse and those who are in strictly monogamous relationships are not at risk unless intravenous drug use is involved. In other words, any sex that involves the exchange of body fluids, except between mutually monogamous couples, may be dangerous behavior. For those who participate in more casual sexual activity, many public health officials recommend the use of condoms to reduce the risk of contracting and/or spreading AIDS.

Surgeon General Koop urges that boys should be told at a very young age about the dangers of rectal (anal) intercourse so that they are not tempted to experiment with this kind of behavior. He warns against sex with prostitutes because they are often infected from needles or previous sexual partners.

The effectiveness of condoms in preventing the transmission of the AIDS virus is not 100 percent. Condoms have a 10 percent failure rate in preventing pregnancy, and the AIDS virus is much smaller than sperm. New laboratory studies appear to confirm the theory that the AIDS virus does not pass through condoms, but a laboratory study differs from real-life situations. Anyone who considers the use of condoms to avoid getting AIDS must consider this 10 percent, or greater, risk of exposure to the AIDS virus. This can be a life or death situation, but 90 percent protection is certainly better than none; only abstinence is 100 percent safe. Tearing of the condom during vaginal or anal intercourse quite obviously increases the risk.

In attempting to learn more about how AIDS is transmitted, an increasing number of researchers are studying heterosexual transmission in the United States, as well as in other countries where this mode of transmission is the predominant mode. Studies are hampered by the difficulty in obtaining accurate information. For example, in Project Aware, a study at San Francisco General Hospital, skilled members of the hospital staff went out into the community to enroll prostitutes and other promiscuous women in their program. Some of the women who agreed to cooperate reported as many as 1,000 sexual contacts a year. Since transmission from female to male has been established, there is increased concern about growing heterosexual transmission in the United States.

In June 1986, in St. Paul, Minnesota, two women who belonged to clubs where male and female members were promiscuous were discovered to be infected with AIDS. Federal health researchers were surprised to learn that most club members were unaware that their sexual practices placed them in a high-risk category for contracting AIDS.

Many drug addicts are well aware that AIDS is spread through intravenous injections as well as through sexual contacts. Preventing AIDS is not the only reason for avoiding such drug abuse, but it is an important one. As of 1986, half of the addicts in New York City were reported to be infected with the virus, and the disease was being spread among intravenous drug abusers across the nation. Although drug addicts have become more aware of the risk of AIDS in the past few years and are reported to be seeking out new needles for injecting their drugs, dealers have been known to repackage used needles and to sell them as new. The increased appearance of AIDS among intravenous drug users has resulted in a number of controversies about the value of providing known addicts with new needles in exchange for old ones. This is a way to bring the addicts to centers where they can be counseled about their problems. Unfortunately, funding for treatment programs is insufficient to help a large percentage of the addicts who want treatment. It has been suggested that increased financing of programs would be much less expensive than caring for people with AIDS.

It has also been pointed out that drug abusers spread AIDS more rapidly than homosexuals because of greater carelessness about transmitting the disease to one another and because infected women can give birth to children who are infected with AIDS. In 78 percent of the cases of AIDS in children, at least one parent is known to have been an intravenous drug user.

Many reports indicate that AIDS is usually spread by more than a tiny amount of the virus. People unfamiliar with the drug scene have asked how the spread could be so great when only a small amount of blood would be transferred by reuse of a needle. Actually, many addicts frequent "shooting galleries" where they go to share equipment. The same needle may be used for as many as 50 injections and in many cases, blood is drawn back into the syringe in an effort to flush out any remaining drug. A significant amount of virus can be transferred this way.

Blood from infected addicts, homosexuals, and others with AIDS was collected by blood banks long before there was any knowledge of AIDS, and tests that make it possible to screen the blood of donors for AIDS antibodies only became available in April 1985. Today, all blood is screened, and the blood supply is considered almost 100 percent safe. However, some people who earlier received blood containing the virus are just beginning to show symptoms of AIDS. "Look back programs" have helped to locate the people who received contaminated blood. In New York City, blood bank officials believe that as many as 500 to 700 patients might have received blood with the AIDS virus between 1977 and 1985. They have been tracing as many as 6,800 recipients nationwide.

Unfounded fears of getting AIDS from donating blood caused a national blood shortage across the United States before media ads spread the word that it was impossible to get AIDS by giving blood.

Only a small percentage of the known cases of AIDS came from transfused blood, and many of these people suffer from hemophilia, a blood clotting disorder. Today, people with this and other diseases requiring transfusions are assured of a safe blood supply.

A small percentage of people who anticipate surgery store their own blood, both for protection against AIDS and because there is less chance of catching other infectious diseases, such as hepatitis. People with rare blood types have done this for years. In some hospitals, designated blood programs are available, in which blood from friends and relatives is stored for a patient.

Reported Adult Cases of AIDS, by Patient Group United States, 1981 to October 20, 1986

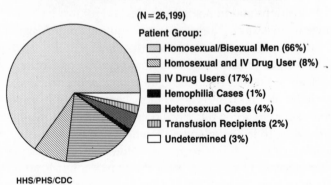

(N = 26,199)

Patient Group:

☐ Homosexual/Bisexual Men (66%)
▨ Homosexual and IV Drug User (8%)
☰ IV Drug Users (17%)
■ Hemophilia Cases (1%)
■ Heterosexual Cases (4%)
▥ Transfusion Recipients (2%)
☐ Undetermined (3%)

HHS/PHS/CDC

However, with the present safety of the blood supply, this is often discouraged. Some experts estimate that the chance of getting AIDS from a transfusion today is about 1 in 250,000.

What about direct transfer of AIDS from human bites? This question has often been raised in connection with permitting children with AIDS to attend school.

A report of a case of a person being bitten by someone with AIDS appeared in the Journal of the American Medical Association (November 7, 1986). On March 28, 1985, a cashier in a grocery store responded to an urgent cry for help at the back of the store. Seeing a man writhing on the floor, the cashier put her fingers in his mouth so that he could not bite his tongue during the seizure. Suddenly, the man's jaw jerked shut and he unconsciously bit her index finger. The wound bled profusely, but no stitches were needed.

Later, it was learned that the man had AIDS. Since the virus that causes the disease has been found in saliva and is known to be transmitted through open wounds, there was concern about whether the virus had been spread to the woman. The man who had suffered the seizure died in November 1985. The grocery cashier, who was tested every other month for eighteen months following the accident, showed no signs of infection from the virus during that time. Since the incubation period ranges from a few months to five or six years, this was not proof positive, but it does appear unlikely that there was transmission of the disease. Because no one knows whether or not the AIDS virus was present in the saliva of the man who had the seizure, the failure of the cashier to contract AIDS does not prove that the virus is not spread through saliva-to-blood contact, but this case is considered as further evidence that there is a low risk of infection from saliva.

When it was first announced that the virus was found in both saliva and tears of some people with AIDS, public concern about mingling with infected people increased. Actresses refused to accept parts in which they would have to kiss men who were admitted or suspected homosexuals. Behavior at Hollywood parties appeared to change with fewer welcome and goodbye kisses among hosts, hostesses, and guests, even though experts assured people that the disease could not be transmitted by pecks on the cheek. Subsequent research has shown that the virus is rarely present in tears or saliva, and when it is, the quantity is probably too small to play a role in infection. However, as a precaution, public health experts still warn about deep kissing with an infected person, and they advise special procedures for dentists and health workers in the field of eye care who are regularly exposed to saliva and tears.

Although much remains to be learned about how AIDS is spread, enough is known to prevent a catastrophe if people avoid dangerous behaviors. Dr. Frank Press, President of the National Academy of Sciences, warns that by 1990 we will lose as many Americans each year to AIDS as we did in the entire Vietnam War. No one really knows what the future will bring, but the picture is bleak, with as many as half of those now infected with the virus likely to develop AIDS within ten years. Perhaps the number will be even greater. But advice on how to avoid AIDS is here today.

5

Plagues in Other Times

Although AIDS is not expected to become another plague like the Black Death that decimated the population in the Middle Ages, many people consider that it fulfills the dictionary definition of plague: an epidemic disease of high mortality.

Infectious diseases caused by microbes have plagued higher organisms ever since living creatures have existed on earth. For example, a twenty-one-million-year-old reptile fossil was found to have suffered from chronic infection of the spine. Many prehistoric animal remains show evidence of disease. There is no doubt that prehistoric man became ill from infections of various kinds. The first recorded epidemic may have occurred as early as 3180 B.C. in Egypt, although there is some dispute about the translation of the record.

In the fifteenth century B.C., there was almost certainly an epidemic in Egypt, as described in the Old Testament in the Book of Exodus: The water of the river turned to blood, the fish died, and the river became foul, so the Egyptians could not drink the water. Then came a plague of frogs, which swarmed over the land; when they died, the land stank from their decaying bodies. Next came lice, which infested both man and beast. Flies, hail, locusts, murrain (a disease of cattle), darkness, boils affecting animals and people, and the death of the first-born followed. "And it came to pass . . . that Jehovah smote all the first-born in the land of Egypt, from the first-born of the Pharaoh . . . unto the first-born of the captive that was in the dungeon, and all the first-born of cattle. . . . There was a great cry in Egypt, for there was not a house where there was not one dead." Clearly this is the story of a series of natural disasters followed by an epidemic that struck down the Egyptians.

Other plagues are described in the Old Testament, but the accounts do not yield enough clues to make exact identification of the diseases involved. However, the Book of Samuel gives an account that may be the earliest description of the bubonic plague, more than three thousand years ago. Because the Philistines had seized the ark of God, God "smote the men of the city, both small and great, and they had emerods in their secret parts." Although there is some controversy as to what emerods were, the Hebrew word means swelling. Accounts of plague throughout history have emphasized swellings in the groin. The association of plague with rats was also noted in ancient writings, although the writers in those times had no idea that the rats carried bubonic plague. In fact, not until the end of the last century was the means of transmission of the plague clarified.

We now know that bubonic plague is caused by a microscopic organism called *Yersinia* (formerly *Pasteurella*) *pestis,* which infects wild rodents. It is transmitted from rodent to rodent and to man by means of the rat flea. The disease is widespread in more than two hundred species of rodents throughout the world. While people sometimes contract plague through contact with wild rodents and their fleas, most outbreaks among humans have occurred when the infection spread to domestic rats. Overcrowding and poor sanitation provide the opportunity for the rat fleas to attack humans.

Although the fleas prefer to feed on rats, they attack humans if rats are not available. So epidemics are most likely to start when the rat hosts die and the fleas migrate to human beings. The flea is infected when it ingests the blood of an animal carrying the plague bacilli in its bloodstream. The bacilli then multiply in the intestinal tract of the flea; when the flea bites another rat or a person, it regurgitates some of the infected material into its host.

Bubonic plague is generally not spread from human to human by fleas, but it is spread when a plague victim develops pneumonia and the organisms are spread by the airborne route.

At least three epidemics of bubonic plague have occurred. The first authentic epidemic was recorded in the sixth century A.D., the second in the fourteenth century, and the last in the late nineteenth century.

The first epidemic, the plague of Justinian, was described by the writer Procopius, who lived at that time. It began in Egypt and spread over the whole known world, penetrating remote regions and killing millions over a period of sixty years. Procopius wrote that phantoms appeared in human form and struck people by a blow, killing them. Some locked themselves in their houses, but the phantoms spoke to them or appeared in dreams, saying they had been selected for death. The plague in Byzantium killed as many as ten thousand people a day. There was a shortage of gravediggers; corpses were piled up in forts or were placed on ships and sent out to sea. Cities and towns were abandoned as some people died and others fled to the countryside. Agriculture was disrupted, resulting in famine, and the entire Roman world became disorganized.

The second epidemic, known as the Black Death, spread to Europe from Asia and the Near East aboard some Genoese trading ships. When they docked in Messina, Sicily, in 1347, the sailors were dead or dying. They had egg-sized swellings called buboes, which oozed blood and pus, on their groins and under their arms, boils spread over their bodies, black blotches appeared on their skin, and they vomited or coughed up blood. They suffered severe pain, fever, and chills, and their bodies smelled foul.

Bubonic plague spread rapidly, killing 90 percent of its victims. Most died within a week, but others, who probably had the more severe pneumonic type of the disease, died within a day. People went to bed well and died in their sleep. Bodies accumulated so rapidly that graveyards were filled, corpses thrown into rivers, mass burial pits were dug, and the dead lay piled up in the streets. People died without last rites and were buried without funeral services. An English bishop gave permission for people to confess to each other if no priest could be found. Pope Clement VI granted remission of sin to everyone who died of the plague, and he even consecrated the Rhone River so that bodies could be dumped in it.

Everyone expected to die, and many believed that the end of the world had come. People were so terrified of being infected that they fled from each other. Accounts of the time related that parents even abandoned their own sick children. The rich fled from the cities and isolated themselves in their country houses; the poor, who lived in crowded, unsanitary conditions in the cities, were more susceptible and died in greater numbers. Peasants died, farms went untended, food stores were depleted, and the population was so decimated that there were not enough people left to do essential work. Government officials died, and lawlessness and chaos increased.

The terrors of the bubonic plague were multiplied by ignorance of the cause. Stinking poisonous mists released after the earthquake of 1348 and mysterious fires were blamed. Medicine in the Middle Ages relied on astrological theories, and the medical faculty of the University of Paris published a learned report that referred to a triple conjunction of Saturn, Jupiter,

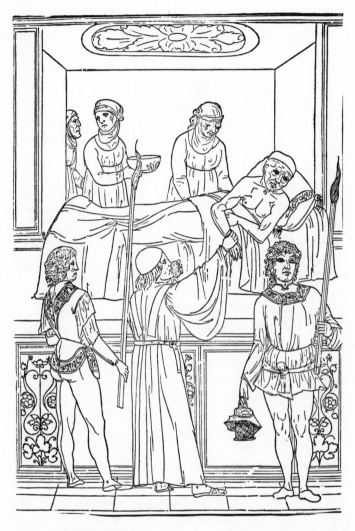

Visit to a Plague Patient, woodcut by Bellini, 1493, shows a doctor risking infection to treat a victim of the Black Death. The doctor holds to his nose a vinegar-soaked sponge, while attendants wave fumigating torches.

and Mars in the fortieth degree of Aquarius as the cause. Most people believed that God had sent the plague as punishment and tried to appease His wrath by various means. This belief led to the rise of the Flagellants, a group of devout Christians who marched through the streets performing rituals of atonement that involved praying and beating themselves with spiked whips. When it became apparent that they were not halting the spread of disease, but fostering it, as well as usurping the power of the clergy, the Pope forbade them to continue.

Demons and spirits were also blamed. The Scandinavians thought that a plague virgin in the form of a blue flame emerged from the mouths of the dead and infected others. Earthquakes, flood, rains of snakes and frogs, locusts, famine, and war were regarded as precursors of the plague. Thousands of European Jews were massacred because of the persistent belief that they poisoned the wells of the Christians, as mentioned earlier.

Some people thought that avoiding excesses and living moderately would protect them; others believed that drinking, carousing, and indulging themselves in every way would prevent disease. The physicians were of little help, and their main treatment was to prescribe the burning of aromatic substances to keep the air pure. People carried pomanders, or spice balls, and sprinkled the floor with rose water.

Pope Clement's doctor made him spend the summer isolated in his apartment, sitting between two large fires. This remedy was probably effective, because it kept the Pope away from people, and the heat kept the fleas away. Other remedies included bleeding, purging, and lancing or cauterizing the buboes. Exotic medicines of rare herbs or powdered gems as well as offensive and disgusting remedies like goat dung, urine, dried lizards, and pus from plague boils were prescribed. Some people believed that inhaling the foul air of the public latrines would protect them.

No amount of praying, atonement, or exotic remedies could protect anyone against the ravages of the Black Death. It recurred several times in the next fifty years, and by the end of the fourteenth century, it had killed off perhaps as many as seventy-five million people, half the population of Europe.

Syphilis appeared in Europe at the end of the fifteenth century, but no one knows how the epidemic originated. In 1676, Richard Weisman, an English surgeon, wrote in his *Severall Chirurgicall Treatises* that there was a venereal disease phobia in England; despite reassurances that they did not have syphilis, many people kept seeking one doctor after the other, "the imagination in which the disease was seated remaining still uncured . . . till they have ruined both their Bodies and their Purses."

Four great cholera epidemics killed millions of people during the nineteenth century. In 1831, the peasants in Hungary revolted because they thought that the cholera was caused by some evil force that the rich were using against them. In 1849, John Snow, an Englishman, was the first to state that cholera was caused by drinking contaminated water and not by miasmic vapors or supernatural forces. He discovered that most of the people who had died in London at that time had drunk Thames River water, which smelled and tasted of sewage. When the handle of the pump was removed, at Snow's suggestion, the epidemic ended shortly. The devastating cholera epidemics did have one good result: people began to realize the importance of good sanitation.

One of the worst epidemics in history was the influenza epidemic of 1918, which killed more than forty million people worldwide. In Philadelphia, some were so fearful of contracting the flu that they fled from visiting nurses making their rounds. In San Francisco, everyone was required to wear a mask.

The polio epidemics in the 1940s brought about similar reactions. Children were quarantined, schools delayed opening, pools and movies were closed, and DDT was sprayed to kill flies,

Some diseases are new; others have been here for a long time, but have not been identified until recently. One such disease is toxic shock syndrome, which appeared in 1978 and was linked to the use of highly absorbent tampons. It was found to be caused by a form of staphylococcus. One epidemiologist at the U.S. Centers for Disease Control believes that in the past, it may have been misdiagnosed as scarlet fever, which has similar symptoms. The offending tampons were taken off the market; while the number of cases has dropped, some are still being reported. The disease may be very old. Some American researchers believe that influenza and toxic shock syndrome may have caused the fall of Athens in 430 to 427 B.C. This epidemic killed tens of thousands of Athenians and so weakened the city-state that it was defeated by Sparta in the Peloponnesian War. The toxic shock syndrome of ancient times may not have been identical to the toxic shock syndrome of modern times, but it is possible that the disease never became extinct.

In 1976 an "explosive" outbreak of severe respiratory illness occurred among delegates attending an American Legion convention in Philadelphia. It became known as Legionnaires' disease. At first, no agent could be identified, either toxic or infective, but it was later found that at least two hundred and twenty cases of pneumonia, thirty-four of them fatal, resulted from a common source of air-borne infection. The cause was found to be a "new" bacterium, previously unknown. However, it was subsequently identified in samples stored in laboratories at the Centers for Disease Control taken during other outbreaks of respiratory illness. By using new techniques, researchers were able to demonstrate that the unexplained pneumonias in outbreaks of illness in 1965, 1968, and 1973, had all been caused by this same bacillus or its close relatives.

Many diseases that appear to be new are not. With improved technology, better reporting of outbreaks, and painstaking detective work in tracking down disease, scientists are better able to identify accurately hitherto uncertain causes of illness.

Although not as worrisome as AIDS, another seemingly new

disease is Brazilian purpuric fever, caused by a mutation of a strain of bacterium that is already known to cause disease in people. Genetic alteration made the organism more virulent, and the disease has a high mortality rate. Even with antibiotic treatment, half the victims have died. Without treatment, all would die. So far, only seventy cases of this new disease have been reported in Brazil, but it could become a serious epidemic.

While scientists do not fear that Brazilian purpuric fever, AIDS, or any other disease will spread as rapidly as the plagues of ancient times, there are many unknowns. Despite increased knowledge about the cause, methods of transmission, and prevention of AIDS, many people have reacted to it in much the same way that people reacted to the Black Death. When there are uncertainties and no absolute answers, many succumb to the fear and superstition that produce a "plague mentality."

6

AIDS International

Perhaps no one will ever know where AIDS began, but it seems likely that Africa was its cradle. According to one theory, a virus that affects African green monkeys may have mutated in such a way that it could attack humans. According to Dr. Myron Essex, of the Harvard School of Public Health, a mechanism may have evolved in these monkeys to control the virus that infects them, so that they remain perfectly healthy. In some parts of Africa, green monkeys hang around parks and picnic areas, where they scavenge food and may bite people. Dr. Essex and his colleagues discovered that about 70 percent of the African green monkeys studied in the laboratory showed signs of infection with a virus closely related to the one that is the basic cause of AIDS in humans. He reported on his work with green monkeys at the international conference on AIDS in April 1985. In the next year, several other related viruses were identified in Africa.

Epidemiologists at Harvard and the New England Regional Primate Center in Massachusetts had suspected that the human

AIDS epidemic originated in central Africa. They looked for AIDS-type viruses in baboons, chimps, and monkeys that came from that part of the world. Seventy-five percent of the thirty monkeys they studied gave evidence of having been infected by a type of virus similar to HIV. Although the simian (relating to monkeys and apes) virus is slightly different from the human virus, some researchers have been successful in infecting chimpanzees with a disease very similar to AIDS.

Some Old World monkeys in both Massachusetts and California primate centers are believed to have suffered from a disease resembling AIDS. Scientists at the New England Primate Center in Massachusetts isolated the virus that caused their illness and noted that it had some striking similarities to the human AIDS virus. The monkeys suffered an immune-deficiency syndrome similar to the syndrome in humans, and they were dying.

No one really knows where the new disease came from, but Dr. Robert Gallo, co-discoverer of HIV, has reported that simian AIDS, or SAIDS, is quite different from AIDS in its mode of attack. Human AIDS virus seems more closely related to leukemia viruses in cows and cats than to the virus that causes the disease in monkeys and chimpanzees. Certainly, human AIDS is a new disease.

AIDS is now present in more than eighty countries. One tenth of the population of central Africa may carry AIDS. Two diseases associated with it in the United States and Europe, Kaposi's sarcoma and Burkitt's lymphoma, are native to central Africa. Dr. Frederick P. Siegal, an authority on AIDS, has suggested that both these diseases may really be manifestations of AIDS in tropical countries where good medical care is not available to large numbers of people. Many who suffer from severely deficient immune systems in tropical countries may die before their diseases are recognized. If AIDS or AIDS-related diseases are native to tropical countries, large numbers of people there may have built up an immunity to the virus.

Although the true global interconnection of AIDS may never

be known, many people believe it began in Africa, was spread to the United States by way of the Caribbean, and then found its way to Europe. Certainly, people seem to want to blame the origin of a disease on some country other than their own. This was the case with syphilis. When syphilis was first encountered at the end of the fifteenth century, the Italians called it the French disease. The French blamed syphilis on the Italians. Columbus and his sailors were said to have brought the disease back from Hispaniola (now Haiti) where they were infected by the natives.

Many Africans were angered by people who attributed the origin of AIDS to them. This prompted the following response from William A. Haseltine, of the Dana Farber Cancer Institute, Harvard Medical School, and School of Public Health in Congressional testimony:

"It is also the natural human response to hope that we ourselves will be spared from this disease. We can tell ourselves that the disease happens to others but may not happen to us. Albert Camus provided a searing description of this mentality in *The Plague.* He writes that at first people thought the disease was only a problem for rats, then for the dirty people who lived across town. Fear came home when death visited next door.

"What many interpret as homophobia [negative attitudes toward homosexuals] regarding AIDS problems may be that. But also at work is a desire to define any group as 'them,' not us. It is becoming increasingly more difficult to define those with AIDS as 'them.' 'Them' now includes not only Africans, not only homosexuals, not only Haitians, not only drug abusers, not only hemophiliacs, but also soldiers and Johns [men who have sex with prostitutes] or Johns' wives. I am confident that we will awaken to realize what problem is in our midst, but when? And how late in the day will that be?"

Until recently, access to accurate information about AIDS in Africa was impossible. In Zaire, where it is believed thousands of people will have died from AIDS by the end of 1986, not one case of AIDS had been reported to the World Health Organization. Researchers studying the problem of AIDS in Central Africa report that changing attitudes about multiple sex partners, including prostitutes, will be a monumental task. Some Africans infected with AIDS have been reported to have had an average of thirty-two sexual partners as compared to three partners for Africans in a control group of uninfected people. Even early studies that cited heterosexual contact as probably the primary mode of transmission of the AIDS virus pointed out that AIDS patients in Central Africa were far more likely than noninfected people to have a history of multiple heterosexual partners and visits to prostitutes. Blood transfusions and unsterile needles used by health workers probably added to the problem. In November 1986, *Newsweek* reported that 10 per— cent of the blood stocks in Zambia were contaminated with AIDS, so patients having a transfusion had a one-in-ten chance of getting AIDS.

Some of the diseases that accompany AIDS in Africa are different from those that accompany AIDS in the United States, but many are common to both areas. A new wasting syndrome that is found in many people with AIDS was first described in Uganda as slim disease. It is now widespread. Symptoms include extreme weight loss, recurrent fevers, and diarrhea. In some people, other infections characteristic of AIDS are also present.

Does the heterosexual spread of AIDS in Africa portend rampant heterosexual transmission in the United States? This question holds much interest for researchers, some of whom emphasize the importance of education to prevent such a problem.

Since about half the cases of AIDS in some parts of Africa occur in women in their reproductive years, it is not surprising to learn that the rate of AIDS in children is high. In one study in Rwanda, children made up a third of the cases. Some of the pediatric cases have been attributed to the practice in many medical clinics of reusing needles without sterilizing them. Boys and girls are inoculated for childhood diseases in groups in many African villages and a single syringe is commonly used for the whole group. The virus from one infected child could reach many this way.

Ed Hooper, a freelance writer in Uganda, reported to *The New York Times* in October 1986 about conditions in the African village of Kyebe, which is being devastated by AIDS. He described a twenty-three-year-old woman whose baby had died from slim disease the week before his visit. Clearly, the mother, who looked elderly in spite of her age, was dying. A boy of fourteen told Mr. Hooper that he was the only one in his family who was still alive; his mother, father, sister, and four brothers had all died from slim disease. Burials seem to go on and on in this area, a place that is known as a danger zone. At first, the people blamed the disease on witchcraft, but they have now accepted the fact that sexual contact is the main means of spreading it.

Health experts have questioned the possibility of the spread of AIDS virus by insects, but studies have found no evidence for this. In Africa, many women are circumcised, but exploration of this theory did not result in positive findings either.

Underreporting of AIDS in Africa is thought to be extensive. There are various reasons for the lack of information; the possible effect on the tourist industry and the future of foreign investment, both of which are important sources of income, have been blamed. Another reason is thought to be anger that the world is blaming Africa for an epidemic that is affecting everyone. Although this fear of admitting the extent of AIDS in African countries is understandable, it makes an already difficult problem even worse. However, toward the end of 1986, some African nations began opening the door to international AIDS researchers.

In addition to learning more about why AIDS is spread primarily by heterosexual intercourse in Africa, health workers can give advice on ways to prevent the further spread of AIDS there. In November 1986, representatives from thirty-seven nations in Africa and around the world participated in a conference sponsored by the World Health Organization. Some of the steps to combat the spread of AIDS discussed at the meeting included encouraging doctors to provide sex education to patients, developing new ways to handle laboratory tests, forming national AIDS committees to encourage widespread education and better health measures, and educating all health workers about AIDS. Women identified as carriers will be discouraged from having children. The World Health Organization told the African nations that it has the funds and the strategy to assist in their battle against AIDS. In countries where financial resources are limited and other diseases, such as malaria, take millions of lives each year, help from the World Health Organization is sorely needed.

Haitians believe they have been unjustly blamed for introducing AIDS to the United States. Some Haitian doctors claim that the disease was brought to Haiti in the first place by American tourists. In his book, *AIDS: The Mystery and the Solution,* Dr. Alan Cantwell cites a case of Georges, a French geologist, who appears to have contracted AIDS while working in Haiti some years before the disease was diagnosed in the United States. Georges was in a serious automobile accident there about eight months after he left France in 1978. He received eight units of Haitian blood, and when he recovered from his injuries, he returned to France.

By 1982, Georges was suffering from diarrhea, abdominal pain, and fever, and he had lost twenty-two pounds. When the diagnosis of AIDS was made, Georges found it difficult to believe that he had a disease most often contracted by homosexual men and drug users. He was married, had a child, never took drugs, and had always been healthy. However, he suffered multiple infections and, by 1983, he had a stroke, a brain abscess caused by a parasite, and high fevers. He finally drifted into a coma and died. Although Georges died four years after his blood transfusions in Haiti and did not become ill until three years after the transfusions, doctors believe the virus was introduced through the Haitian blood bank. No case seems to have been traced and recorded of AIDS having been brought into Haiti in the same way, though it has no doubt happened more than once.

About the time that AIDS was first recognized in the United States, doctors reported detecting the disease in some Haitians who had recently immigrated. Since this was a highly publicized and easily studied group, and since medical checking of immigrants was routine, reporters seized on the situation. The media stated that some "boat people" were thought to have died from AIDS en route, while other showed symptoms when they arrived. Haitians who had been in the United States for as long as ten years also showed AIDS symptoms. Observers leaped to the unfounded conclusion that a genetic factor might make Haitians particularly susceptible to AIDS, but this was found to be an incorrect and unfair assumption.

Medical investigators from the Centers for Disease Control and the University of Miami Medical School went to Port-au-Prince, the capital of Haiti. Doctors from Cornell University were already in the country studying tropical diseases. Together they found that the first cases of AIDS-related diseases appeared in 1979. By 1983, it had been established that most AIDS cases were related to sexual contact, but by then Haitians as a group had been unfairly stigmatized because of the early reports.

At one time certain voodoo practices had been suspected of spreading AIDS among Haitians, since these rituals may involve mixing of blood, scarring of skin, and cutting of flesh with knives that might often be unsterile. But it has since been shown that there is no connection between animal fever, voodoo rituals not involving transfer of blood, and AIDS.

Because Haiti was a popular vacation spot for homosexual men before AIDS was well known, there was speculation about whether tourists had picked up AIDS on the island or whether they might have taken the disease there. Certainly, there were "social clubs" in Haiti, as in many other countries, where prostitution and unusual sexual practices may have played a part in the spread of the disease. But there was no evident connection between these activities and the many immigrants to the United States who suffered from AIDS.

Imagine a frightened, sick young man who has just come to the United States from Haiti. He is being examined by a doctor who does not speak his language. The doctor asks the Haitian if he is a homosexual or if he has used narcotics intravenously, but the Haitian cannot understand the questions. Then a doctor who speaks French interviews him. The patient's native language is Creole, but he understands some French. He hears the questions, "Do you shoot drugs?" "Are you a homosexual?" and he answers in the negative to both questions. Although the diagnosis appears to be AIDS, the doctors wonder how the man has contracted the disease.

Investigations of the Haitian connection with AIDS have unveiled the strong cultural taboo against homosexuality that led to denial by many Haitians with AIDS. It accounted for the possibility that men who supported families by prostitution may have spread it to their wives, which would explain the large percentage of Haitian women with AIDS. Study of the culture also revealed that folk doctors sometimes use the same needles for injecting medicines over and over again, another method of spreading disease. Such information led to the elimination of Haitians from the list of those inherently at high risk of being infected with AIDS.

Haitians feel that bad publicity about their country in placing it on the high-risk list for AIDS was responsible for a decrease of tourism. Many Haitians living abroad were hurt because they were unjustly singled out as having a high incidence of AIDS.

Haiti is still of special interest to researchers who are looking for more answers about the mode of transmission. Studies show a rate of one case in women for each case in men in Haiti. Although this ratio is lower for women than in Africa, it is much greater than in the United States and Europe.

In Europe, where the disease appears to spread in a way similar to that in the United States, there are relatively fewer people with AIDS. Most reported cases appear among homosexuals and intravenous drug abusers.

Medical workers in India have long feared the introduction of AIDS. In 1986, when a small number of cases were reported there, they faced the moment of truth. Special concerns about AIDS in India stem from the knowledge that AIDS appears to spread quickly in poverty areas. India has a huge population, much of it crowded together, through which the disease could spread. Doctors in India already have a difficult time coping with other diseases, such as malaria, cholera, and tuberculosis.

In Southeast Asia, AIDS has reached some homosexuals and some prostitutes in the cities. The potential for widespread infection is there, too.

Certainly, AIDS is an international disease. International travelers should be cautious about medical care that involves intravenous injections and/or blood transfusions in countries where blood is not screened for AIDS. In many of the developing countries, it is customary to give medications by injection both in pharmacies and in clinics. Travelers must consider the fact that syringes and other medical equipment may not be sterilized and may be a source of the AIDS virus.

7

An Epidemic of Fear

While AIDS may be considered an epidemic in the medical sense because there has been an unexpected increase in the incidence of the disease, it has caused a much larger epidemic of fear. One woman, who had no knowledge of how AIDS is transmitted, felt especially threatened by the disease. She suggested that all people with AIDS be made to wear the letter A on their chests, much as adulteresses were forced to do many years ago in Puritan colonies.

Some people are so frightened by AIDS that they shun all homosexuals. Many customers have changed hairdressers because they suspected that the ones they frequented were gay. They now insist on women doing their hair. Actresses have refused to be made up by men who might be homosexual. One couple visiting New Orleans was so concerned about the numerous gay waiters in the French Quarter restaurants that they stopped going out to eat. They bought food in supermarkets and ate it in their hotel room. A woman who was given a book purchased at a gay-lesbian book store called the store and asked if she could safely open the package without getting AIDS. Even people who do not think they know a homosexual person have expressed fear of the disease. All of these people were acting on unfounded fears.

In spite of assurances in the media that AIDS cannot be spread by casual contact, people continue to express concern about acquiring the disease when eating in restaurants, working in an office with a homosexual, and just breathing the same air as someone in a high-risk group.

Even people who feel they should know better often show some fear of this new and somewhat mysterious disease. Not long after Mary had read an article about the terrible wasting away of an AIDS patient before his death, she was assigned to write an article on the subject that involved interviewing a homosexual. She had no reason to believe that he had the disease, but she backed away from him when he mentioned that a number of his friends had died from AIDS. Mary knew that the disease could not be spread through the air when the man coughed. However, she could not help feeling uncomfortable about being near him. She remembered she had felt that people who were afraid to work with AIDS victims were foolish, but the irrational feeling was there.

Fear of AIDS became widespread in the summer of 1985. In Louisville, Kentucky, police officers wore rubber gloves as a precaution against AIDS when they checked for underage drinkers at a bar patronized mainly by homosexuals. They explained that they had to search pockets and the groin area when they made an arrest. Although there is no evidence of transmission from such procedures, the rubber gloves made them feel safer.

By 1985, many homosexual partners of men who had developed AIDS were complaining about being asked by their landlords to vacate their apartments. Men with AIDS were exposed to further suffering at their jobs, where other workers made them feel isolated. Some AIDS victims reported that co-workers would not use the same water fountain, the phones, or computer terminals where they worked. One man reported that he was asked to work at home, then offered a private office. When he refused both of these requests, he was given a heavier work load. He claims his supervisor threatened to give him a poor evaluation because he could not keep up. At that point, the company offered him retirement with full medical benefits. He accepted this because he was afraid of being fired and losing everything.

No matter how often public health officials insist that casual person-to-person contact appears to pose no risk, fears reach panic proportions in some communities. Frightened people have pointed out that asbestos was once considered safe and used in many schoolrooms. Today, asbestos is being removed from the schoolrooms because of evidence that exposure to asbestos can play a part in causing cancer. They ask, "Will the experts someday discover that they were wrong when they claim that one cannot contract AIDS by working next to a person who is suffering from the disease?"

The epidemic of fear has been evident in many places. Some television technicians refused to work on a program in which an AIDS patient was to be interviewed. Fourteen people asked to be excused from jury duty in the trial of a man who had AIDS and was accused of murder. The sheriff's deputies who had to walk with this murder suspect were so concerned about contracting the disease that they wore rubber gloves and other protective clothing when they escorted him into the courtroom.

A Vermont woman who took in two male boarders saw them leaving the bathroom together. She burned the bedsheets they had used and called the AIDS hotline to ask if she had been infected by the virus.

Rumors that people should not eat in restaurants where food was cooked or served by homosexuals began when it was suggested that the cook might drop tears into the food while peeling onions and the tears might contain the AIDS virus. The virus has been found in the tears of people with AIDS, but in very small amounts. Besides, no one has ever been known to contract AIDS from eating the virus.

A prison inmate once laced the coffee of a guard with blood that he believed contained the virus. In another case, a confirmed carrier of AIDS virus spit at some policemen. Although there was some discussion about a trial for attempted murder, that idea was dropped, since AIDS cannot be spread that way.

Suggestions have been made that a good way to scare someone is to put your hand on a person's shoulder, lean over close, and tell the person you have AIDS. For those who have AIDS, this is a sick joke. For those who are frightened by such action, education is needed.

There have been reports that funeral homes refused to handle the bodies of AIDS patients without using elaborate precautions. In one case, it was alleged that a funeral home charged a family an extra two hundred dollars for the gloves and gowns used to handle an AIDS patient's body, and another funeral home tried to sell a family an expensive "germ-free" coffin. A Baltimore man, Don Miller, who is concerned about the rights of homosexuals, reported that he called ninety-nine funeral homes to see what response they gave when he told them he had AIDS and was making funeral arrangements in advance. Ten refused to deal with him, and about half of them said they would require special conditions such as no embalming and/or a sealed casket. Some groups have been working toward establishing guidelines for embalming and burying people who had AIDS.

Children with AIDS and those whose parents have AIDS have been the victims of the epidemic of fear that spread throughout the country. Prospective foster parents often shy away from children whose mothers died from infectious diseases because of AIDS, even though the children do not have the disease. For example, one little boy lived at Jackson Memorial

Reported Cases of AIDS by Age Group, United States 1981 to October 20, 1986

Age Group	Cases	Percentage of Total
<13 Years	367	1
13 - 19	111	0
20 - 29	5,554	21
30 - 39	12,466	47
40 - 49	5,472	21
Over 49	2,596	10
Total	26,566	100

HHS/PHS/CDC

Hospital in Miami, Florida, for two years after he was born because his mother had AIDS before she died. He showed no indication of having the virus.

Publicity about the needs of children whose parents were AIDS sufferers and about those with AIDS and AIDS-related complex has helped to place some of these children in foster homes. Many of them are born to families who are too sick to raise them, so they are abandoned. They may be placed in foster care before their illness is diagnosed, or they may be accepted by foster parents who are willing to care for them in spite of their past or present connection with the disease. Foster parents may shy away from taking these children for two reasons: fear of catching the disease and fear of the emotional trauma that comes with loss of a child in their care.

A child of a drug-addicted mother lived in a hospital for twenty months before a foster mother was found who would accept her after she had been diagnosed as having AIDS-related complex. Her foster mother said her daughter's life might be short, but she wanted her to have the best quality of life possible. However, she found it difficult to place the child in a regular nursery school program because of her disease, even though doctors assured her that the child would not put other children at risk.

Harry Silverstein, the director of placement at the Office of Special Services for Children in New York City, reported the following placement of sixteen AIDS children over a period of two years: three lived with relatives, one returned to a foster family, three were placed after publicity campaigns, two have died and seven remained homeless. The homeless children lived in New York City hospitals, even though they were not sick enough to require hospital care. There was nowhere else for them to go.

One baby born to a mother who died of AIDS is reported to have had so little attention that he showed little reaction to people. When a baby doll was placed next to the child, one physician noted that he could hardly tell the difference between the doll and the child.

Not all children with AIDS are treated so poorly. A volunteer program started by the Gay Men's Health Crisis in New York has succeeded in helping many children who are hospitalized because of AIDS-related illnesses. These volunteers spend time visiting the children, something many of their relatives will not do. They try to bring joy and laughter into the lives of children who are very lonely because they have been ostracized by fear. Many families of a child with AIDS try to keep the diagnosis a secret, since many neighbors will not let their healthy children play with an infected child. The director of the Gay Men's Health Crisis, Dolores Smithies, tells of a boy who often says to her, "Bring me friends."

While some babies die quickly after birth, others live well into school age. In a number of places, hospitals have begun day care programs for children with AIDS, and a California monastery has opened its doors to unwanted infants born with AIDS who might otherwise have to spend their lives in hospitals. For many children with AIDS, life outside the hospital is one in which they are shunned by friends, neighbors, and even relatives because of the fear that still surrounds the disease.

Controversies about whether or not children with AIDS should be permitted to attend school have reached far and wide. The case of Ryan White of Russiaville, Indiana, was well publicized. A hemophiliac, he contracted AIDS from a blood transfusion he received in December 1984. At one point, Ryan was forced to monitor classes at home by telephone because of a restraining order obtained by parents of the other children. In the fall of 1986, Ryan started school with his class for the first time in two years, after the parents who fought his return dropped their lawsuit because of legal costs. Ryan's school had been picketed in the past, but by 1986, some students just took the attitude that they did not mind his being in school as long as he did not sit near them. Ryan was assigned his own bathroom and was given disposable utensils in the cafeteria, even though scientists believe this precaution to be unnecessary. School staff members were instructed in handling any health emergencies that arose.

An eighth grader with AIDS attended junior high school in Swansea, Massachusetts, with permission from the administration and with the support of students. Some of the students not only expressed their willingness to attend school with the student, but approached the principal of the school with plans for a fund-raising drive for research to help find a cure for the disease. However, many parents responded with alarm to having a student with AIDS attending school with their own teenagers, and it was suspected that a number of parents were keeping their sons and daughters from school, despite assurances from health officials and school administrators.

In New York City, when school opened in late August of 1985, the fear of AIDS created a great deal of excitement. Whether or not a child who had AIDS could attend public school in New York City was determined by a panel made up of health experts, an educator, and a parent. One child with AIDS had been attending school for three years and was identified only as a second grader. The child was said to have been born with AIDS but was in good health, the disease being in remission. She had received all the inoculations necessary for school admission, and had recovered from a case of chicken pox, managing to fight off this childhood illness uneventfully.

Although most of the 946,000 children returned to school despite the fact that the AIDS student was attending an unidentified school, 12,000 of the 47,000 students in two school districts in Queens did not attend the first day of school. Mothers and children picketed the schools, carrying placards with slogans such as KEEP AIDS OUT OF PUBLIC SCHOOLS, TEACHERS AIDES NOT STUDENT AIDS, and OUR CHILDREN WANT GOOD GRADES, NOT AIDS. Two thousand fewer students stayed home the second day, while parents demanded that the student be identified and that the names of teachers or other staff members with AIDS be made known. The boycott in Queens was referred to as uninformed hysteria, not reasoned dissent.

While the American Medical Association says that preschoolers with AIDS should not be sent to day-care centers because they may bite and scratch and are not always fully toilet trained, doctors emphasize that school-age children do not pose a threat to their classmates.

In Hollywood, many people were near hysteria after Rock Hudson's announcement that he was suffering from AIDS. Some actresses who had kissed people with AIDS were especially concerned, while others refused to work with anyone considered to be gay. After one actor became sick, make-up artists burned the brushes they had used on him. But Hollywood stars have been outstanding in their support of care for persons with AIDS and research on AIDS. Shortly before he died, Rock Hudson sent a brief message to a benefit dinner, "I am not happy that I am sick. I am not happy that I have AIDS. But if that is helping others, I can, at least, know that my own misfortune has had some positive worth."

Only through education and further research can one strike a balance between fear of the disease, sensible precautions, and concern for people who suffer from AIDS. Fear makes people "block out" information. We need more campaigns which emphasize the lack of danger from casual contact since polls show that people are simply not listening.

8

Medical Progress

The AIDS disease process is enormously complex, but a tremendous amount of progress has been made since its discovery in 1981. Glimmers of hope began to appear by 1986, with the first clinical trials of a drug to prolong the life of people with AIDS. No claims were made for the drug, AZT, as a cure, but it was an early battle won in the war against AIDS.

The question has been asked again and again, "Where did AIDS come from?" and the question may never be definitely answered. Some researchers believe that the AIDS virus may have existed thousands of years ago in pockets of the world where people were not in contact with others. These isolated groups, probably in Africa, may have adapted to living with the virus. But, with the breakdown of tribal and geographical boundaries, previously unexposed people suffered more devastating effects of the virus for which they had no immunity. Another theory suggests that the virus was a variation of one that infected the green monkeys (see p. 46). No matter where it came from, reports of unusual diseases in several parts of the United States surprised doctors and eventually led them to the discovery of what has become known as AIDS. The AIDS puzzle is far from solved, but researchers have made great progress since the time when the disease was first named in 1982. Before that year, reports of unusual diseases in several parts of the United States surprised the doctors and eventually alerted them to the discovery of a new syndrome.

The first well-documented cases of what was later called AIDS were found in San Francisco and New York in 1981. A young male homosexual in San Francisco was found to be suffering from a severe fungal infection to which he had little immune reaction. In fact, his immune system did not appear to respond to any disease. Then, he developed a disease known as *Pneumocystis carinii* pneumonia (PCP), a type of pneumonia that is caused by a parasite. This disease is usually found only among severely malnourished individuals or people whose immune systems have been impaired by drugs such as those used in the treatment of cancer or in connection with organ transplants. The young man died by the end of the year.

About the same time as PCP developed in the San Francisco patient, a dermatologist in New York encountered two cases of Kaposi's sarcoma (KS) in one week, both in young male homosexuals. This disease was rare in the United States, had almost always been mild, and had appeared only in elderly men of Mediterranean descent. A more virulent strain occurred in some young African men, but it was rarely seen in young American men before 1980. The KS seen in young homosexual men was more malignant, quickly spreading through the body, killing a far greater number of men than the usual, more indolent form, which often does not become very invasive.

The two diseases, PCP and KS, were reported to the Centers for Disease Control. By late 1981, five hundred cases of these diseases had been diagnosed in patients who appeared to have an associated severe immune deficiency. Alerted doctors and scientists from the Centers for Disease Control increased their medical detective work. The epidemiologists, whose job it is to study patterns of disease in humans and factors that influence the course of the disease, asked questions of the homosexual community in hopes of finding a link for the unusual diseases that had been reported. They also interviewed every victim of unusual viruses that they could find, tested samples of their blood, urine, saliva, and feces for every known microorganism that might be the cause of their problems. The epidemiologists did not find a particular bacterium, virus, or parasite, but they did learn that the people with the viruses were mostly homosexuals who had been involved with a number of different partners. By 1982, they were also well aware that some of the cases were found in drug abusers, many of whom share needles to inject illegal drugs or use needles that they find on the street or in trash cans.

In the spring of 1982, the Centers for Disease Control received word that a hemophiliac in Miami, Florida, was suffering from PCP, but he died before tests could be made on his immune system. Then, a fifty-nine-year-old man in Denver, Colorado, who was also a hemophiliac, came down with PCP. An investigator from the Centers for Disease Control flew to the hospital in Denver and learned that the man had a suppressed immune system. Hemophiliacs need transfusions of plasma Factor VIII when they suffer from uncontrolled bleeding, and since there is only a minute amount of Factor VIII in the blood of each person, many donors are needed to make up enough of this artificially supplied clotting factor. Many of the donors are students and other young men, some of whom could have been carrying the virus believed to cause the syndrome. As more hemophiliacs developed the problem, the link to blood products was soon established.

By the summer of 1982, someone (it is not certain who) thought of the name, acquired immune deficiency syndrome, and AIDS finally had a name. That the cause of AIDS was something new became increasingly clear. It was not something that human beings had contracted in days gone by, although later search of records by investigators from the Centers for Disease Control showed that the disease had appeared in New York in 1979, and that there had been seven cases that year.

As the investigation gathered momentum, a number of theories were explored, including the possibility of a connection with tanning salons or drugs of abuse known as poppers (amyl or butyl nitrate)—stimulants that are sometimes used to enhance sexual pleasure. After data from two hundred patients was analyzed, it was apparent that AIDS could be transmitted sexually and was probably spread this way in the majority of cases.

When germs or other foreign substances invade the body, the complex immune system is activated in defense. White blood cells called lymphocytes play an important part in this reaction. The lymphocytes known as B-cells produce antibodies to the invading substance, the antigen. Other lymphocytes known as T-cells, of which there are several types, also function as part of the immune system and help eliminate foreign substances. Some types function as helpers or suppressors to coordinate the system and maintain a balance. They cooperate with a number of different kinds of cells in the immune system, keeping it active enough to defend the body against invaders, but not so active that the body damages its own tissues. HIV is thought to be remarkably specific in attacking the protective T-4 lymphocyte cells, and this attack cripples the whole immune system.

In 1984, doctors began to recognize the ability of the AIDS virus to attack the central nervous system. At one time, mental symptoms in AIDS patients were attributed to psychological factors, a response to the stress of having a terminal illness, and to the many infections suffered. About 30 percent of AIDS patients develop psychiatric disorders such as severe depression, suicidal tendencies, and paranoia.

Dr. Robert Gallo of the National Institutes of Health in Bethesda, Maryland, and his research group were among the first to report that the AIDS virus can infect brain cells as well as immune system cells. Dr. Jay A. Levy and his colleagues at the University of California at San Francisco reported finding the AIDS virus, which they call ARV, in the brains and spinal fluid of thirteen AIDS patients.

Autopsies of the brains of some AIDS patients have shown that they are shrunken. At Cornell University, scientists did autopsies on eighty-nine patients who had AIDS and found damage to the brain and spinal cord in twenty of them. Doctors estimate that about 30 percent of AIDS patients show symptoms of brain or spinal cord damage. Symptoms such as memory loss, inability to make decisions, lack of interest in the world around them, and loss of muscle coordination have been attributed to the invasion of the brain and spinal cord by the AIDS virus.

The AIDS virus can cross the blood-brain barrier, a physiological safeguard that protects the brain from most harmful agents that circulate in the blood. This makes the search for a cure more difficult. Because the AIDS virus, unlike most disease-causing organisms, can pass through the cells that line the tiny blood vessels in the central nervous system, scientists must approach the double threat posed by a virus that can attack both the immune system and the brain. Viruses in the brain can find sanctuary from medicines that cannot cross the blood-brain barrier. In other words, the brain and other parts of the central nervous system can act as a reservoir for future infections.

In some cases, the AIDS virus produces illness from brain cell damage before there are signs of trouble with the body's immune system. For example, one woman, a heterosexual in her twenties, appeared at St. Vincent's Hospital and Medical Center in New York City suffering from delusions, auditory hallucinations, hyperactivity, and many neurologic symptoms. She had been in a long-term relationship with a man who was later discovered to

**Reported Cases of AIDS and Case Fatality Rate
by Disease Category, United States
1981 to October 20, 1986**

Disease Category	Cases	Deaths	Case Fatality Rate(%)
Both KS and PCP	1,404	987	70
KS without PCP	4,383	2,041	47
PCP without KS	15,556	8,846	57
Other Opportunistic Diseases	5,223	3,103	59
Total	26,566	14,977	56

HHS/PHS/CDC

be bisexual. The usual medications for this condition only temporarily relieved her symptoms, and, during the next three months, she lost weight, had fevers, and showed other symptoms of AIDS. A month later she developed *Pneumocystis carinii* pneumonia, and two weeks later she developed skin lesions that were diagnosed as Kaposi's sarcoma. It is uncertain whether her mental condition was caused by AIDS or whether the stress of her psychiatric disorder played a part in the development of full-blown AIDS from formerly latent viruses.

The involvement of the central nervous system may be chronic, and it is often difficult for doctors to determine whether a person is suffering from AIDS or from another disease. Many questions about the effect of HIV on the brain remain unanswered, but it appears certain that some people with AIDS suffer brain damage before other symptoms appear. Estimates of those who will suffer damage to the central nervous system during the course of the disease run as high as 50 percent. Some patients with AIDS suffer severe memory loss and personality changes, and it is feared that many more people will have to face these devastating symptoms in the future.

So much has been learned about AIDS in recent years, that the discovery of the virus seems long ago. However, this knowledge came through meticulous work and the cooperation of many scientists. In fact it was isolated in two countries, the United States and France. In May of 1983, a French team under the leadership of Dr. Luc Montagnier of the Institut Pasteur in Paris reported that they had isolated a new virus from a patient with AIDS-related symptoms. They named it lymphadenopathy-asociated virus, or LAV. Early in 1984, Dr. Gallo and his associates reported that they had identified the virus that appeared to cause AIDS, and they had produced it in large quantities. They called it HTLV-III, citing its relationship to HTLV-I and HTLV-II viruses. Later analysis of the genetic structures of these viruses showed LAV and HTLV-III (now called HIV) to be virtually identical.

HTLV-I and HTLV-II differ from HIV in a number of ways. For example, HTLV-I causes some forms of human leukemia and lymphoma. HTLV-II has not been proven to cause any disease, but it was found originally in human cancer tissue. HTLV-I and HTLV-II often cause laboratory cell cultures to multiply without discipline, as in cancer, while HIV kills them, explaining the devastating deterioration of the immune system.

HTLV-IV was discovered by Dr. Myron Essex of the Harvard School of Public Health in 1986 in West Africa. He soon began laboratory experiments with this form of the virus in an effort to see if it produced antibodies in animals that could neutralize the human AIDS virus outside the body. He and other scientists are exploring HTLV-IV's potential in the development of a vaccine.

A vaccine works by tricking the body's immune system into behaving as though it had actually been invaded by a disease-causing virus. This causes the production of antibodies that help the immune system to protect against the invasion of the virus. Antibodies produced by a vaccine circulate in the blood for years, providing long-term protection.

Most familiar vaccines that work against viruses, such as those for mumps and measles, use live viruses that have been weakened in laboratories. People who are vaccinated produce antibodies against the weakened strain and are then protected against the actual disease. In the case of smallpox, vaccination with the cowpox virus was enough to produce antibodies that would defend the body against the more virulent smallpox. Many researchers believe that this kind of vaccine is not suitable for AIDS, because the weakened virus might manage to gain strength in the body, giving rise to AIDS.

Researchers at the Dana-Farber Cancer Institute and the National Cancer Institute announced simultaneously that they could produce intact but dead HIV. These viruses could not reproduce in the laboratory, but much testing remains to be done to make certain that they cannot be reactivated.

Another approach to producing a vaccine is based on genetic engineering. By pinpointing certain genes in the AIDS virus that may be the key to the disease and by substituting or removing them, it might be possible to produce a harmless vaccine. Some researchers have successfully used genetic engineering techniques to modify the smallpox vaccine in such a way that it carries a key gene of the AIDS virus. Proteins that are produced fool the cell into which they are introduced into producing antibodies against the AIDS virus. But many problems remain with this and with other approaches.

The AIDS virus has been called especially diabolic, a problem that can be better understood if one has a general idea of the structure of viruses. Viruses of any kind are unbelievably small; as many as 100,000 could fit on the head of a pin. Some kinds of viruses, including AIDS, develop new strains that can outwit the immune cells that produced antibodies to fight the original invaders in the body.

Viruses are composed of molecules known as DNA (deoxyribonucleic acid) or RNA (ribonucleic acid) surrounded by an envelope, or outer coat of protein. Even though DNA and RNA are forms of genetic material, viruses cannot reproduce by themselves. When they enter cells, they hijack genetic material in the cells and reprogram it in such a way that new viruses are formed. Some of the newly formed viruses escape from the cells, enter more cells, and the disease process continues. Eventually, the cells that have been invaded die and release huge numbers of new viruses. These enter more cells and continue to produce more viruses. The immune system can thus be overwhelmed.

The AIDS virus is one that keeps changing its protein coat. As a result, antibodies generated against one strain of the virus might not recognize the envelope of another strain, giving the new strain a chance to multiply freely. Researchers are exploring the AIDS virus coat through complex techniques in efforts to overcome this problem. Another problem in the battle against AIDS is that human antibodies may not have the ability to cope with the AIDS virus.

All the varieties of vaccines that are produced experimentally need testing, and testing an AIDS vaccine is especially difficult. The logistics and cost of clinical trials and the liability that could be involved make mass immunization an unlikely option for the near future. Some researchers estimate that it could take as long as four years to find out if a vaccine works, because the virus can remain latent for at least that long.

The first drug to receive approval for use by people with AIDS was offered not as a cure, but as one that could help in treating the symptoms of the disease. AZT (azidothymidine) was developed in an effort to inhibit the duplication of cancer cells, but it did not work and was put on the shelf for possible future use. As soon as Dr. Robert Gallo's laboratory was able to make sufficient amounts of the AIDS virus available, researchers began testing drugs to discover an effective weapon against AIDS. At Burroughs-Wellcome laboratories, AZT began showing promise by early 1985. It was made available to patients in November 1986, but along with the promise of this experimental drug came questions of side effects and the possible dangers of long-term use.

The AIDS virus belongs to a group known as retroviruses, whose genetic instructions are in RNA, rather than the more familiar pattern of having them present in DNA. When a retrovirus invades a cell, an enzyme known as reverse transcriptase directs the formation of a DNA molecule. This DNA molecule enters the nucleus of the cell that has been invaded and changes the cell's genetic structure so that new virus particles are formed. Since AZT appears to inhibit reverse transcriptase, it disrupts the chemical chain necessary for the virus to duplicate itself in the human body. The action is complex, but this drug did seem to prolong life in many AIDS victims. Although early results have been promising and the drug does appear to cross the blood-brain barrier, much remains to be learned.

Many different drugs are being explored experimentally in the battle against AIDS, with various degrees of success. But researchers argue that some of the drugs produce such serious side effects that they could cause the death of patients. Even when people with AIDS develop some immunity as measured by antibodies, they continue to carry the virus in some of their cells and they can still spread the disease. This means a drug must be taken throughout the person's life.

While numerous drugs and vaccines are being explored as weapons against AIDS, the greatest hope for control of AIDS still lies in education to prevent its spread. This is the most realistic goal at the present time.

9

AIDS: A Challenge for the Future

What will AIDS mean to you in the future? It may play an important part in the lives of everyone, for it is predicted to be a dominant political, ethical, and economic force in the next decade. Predictions range from a continuing mild epidemic to a catastrophic one. Certainly, complacency about AIDS is dangerous. The alarm button has been pressed, but many people are still not aware of the danger they face. Others panic without cause.

AIDS is expected to be one of the top ten causes of death by 1991, according to a Public Health Service report. The virus that causes AIDS does not discriminate by age, sex, race, or ethnic group; the dangerous behaviors that put one at risk have already been mentioned.

A new concern is a possible silent epidemic among young people. Education, many experts say, must reach out to areas where AIDS transmission among heterosexuals is most likely, including certain larger cities and in high schools and colleges.

While large numbers of people have been frightened about the possibility of receiving infected blood via transfusions, and many have been needlessly concerned about the possibility of getting AIDS by giving blood, blood transfusions have become quite safe. As of April 1986, about 350 cases of AIDS arising from blood transfusions had been reported nationally. However, most of these cases occurred before 1983, when safer methods of checking blood were introduced.

Although the number of cases of AIDS from transfusions of blood and blood products is quite small, the proportion of cases in this group increased between 1983 and 1986. Persons who were infected before the introduction of blood-donor screening are expected to continue to develop AIDS, but the number of transfusion-related AIDS cases should begin to decline by the end of the decade.

As mentioned earlier, the chance of getting infected blood today is considered to be less than 1 in 250,000. An estimated 12 million units of whole blood are donated each year in the United States and about 12,000 of these units are infected with AIDS. Only about one hundred slip through the screening tests because antibodies usually do not develop until about three weeks to three months after a person has been infected with the AIDS virus. A newly infected person could donate blood that would pass through the screening tests.

Blood donations dropped by 10 percent during the early years of the AIDS epidemic, but the message that one cannot get AIDS by donating blood appears to be reaching donors. The Red Cross uses, and always has used, sterilized hypodermic needles. Each is used once and then thrown away. Homosexual and bisexual men have been asked to refrain from giving blood, and each blood donor is asked a series of questions before donating.

In order to ensure that a person is not lying during the screening or possibly is infected without knowing, all the blood is tested. After donations are made, all blood is screened by a test known as ELISA (enzyme-linked immunosorbent assay), and any blood with HIV antibodies is rejected. In March 1985, blood centers began testing all donations. This test, although now used in efforts to screen persons other than blood donors, is not a test for AIDS. When the virus enters the body of a person, the immune system generates specific antibodies for HIV. So, if one has antibodies for HIV, it can be determined that this person has been exposed to the virus. Although this is an indirect test, it works well for blood banks because they can reject blood that is positive for the presence of the antibodies. It says nothing about the status of the person as a carrier of AIDS or of the likelihood of the individual ever developing full-blown AIDS.

ELISA is very sensitive, but it is not always accurate. A small percentage of blood that tested negative during the clinical trials was later shown to have contained the virus HIV. And not all positive tests results are accurate. At least 20,000 people who have tested positive for HIV antibodies in initial screening were negative on more accurate follow-up tests.

Imagine being notified by a blood bank that your blood donation was rejected because you tested positive for HIV. If such is the case you will be asked to take a second ELISA test to confirm the results. If this is also positive, you will be asked to undergo a more technically difficult and more expensive test known as the Western Blot test. This test identifies antibodies to proteins of specific molecular weight. If they find that the results are negative, you can be sure you have not been infected by the virus. If all three tests are positive, the evidence that you have been exposed to HIV is considered conclusive.

Although the ELISA test was developed to screen out contaminated blood that is collected for transfusions at blood banks, the test also identifies people who have been exposed to the virus. Blood banks are not consistent in how they handle notifying those whose tests are positive, but all agree that the names of these people must be kept confidential.

Testing for antibodies has become a controversial issue because of the fear that people who test positive might be exposed. Some groups, such as the Gay Men's Health Crisis in New York City, have advised homosexuals, who are understandably eager to learn whether or not they have been exposed to the AIDS virus, to consider the possible consequences of testing. They warn that any lack of confidentiality could mean the loss of a job or health insurance. Although they point out that a secondary stated use of the testing is to gather data on how widely the infection has spread among the general population and, specifically, among people in high-risk groups, the test makes no predictions. Although testing under special and protected conditions is recommended by the majority of gay organizations, the signing of a so-called informed consent document assuring the maximum protection of test results is also recommended.

As long ago as October 1, 1985, new recruits for the military services had no choice in undergoing testing for the AIDS antibody. Those applicants who test positive in two separate tests are rejected. The Assistant Secretary of Defense for Health Affairs pointed out that new recruits are given routine smallpox vaccinations. People with AIDS would have little defense even against the weak dose of smallpox virus in the vaccine.

On October 18, 1985, the Defense Department moved one step further in their efforts to stop the spread of AIDS in the armed forces. It was announced that all 2.1 million military personnel would be screened for the presence of antibodies to HIV. The Pentagon cited several reasons for this move. For one, all members of the armed forces are considered to be "walking blood banks" in combat and in terrorist situations. Transfusions would increase the risk of infected individuals passing the AIDS virus to other soldiers. Furthermore, the army must be able to deploy personnel anywhere in the world on short notice. Having to be concerned with which people have AIDS would impede combat readiness. The need to quickly immunize soldiers who are to be sent to areas where there are diseases uncommon in the United States also presents a problem. People with immune systems damaged by AIDS are poor candidates for such immunization.

While military officials claim that the policy of testing is needed for good reasons, some critics charge that the action is unjustified on medical grounds and is prompted, at least in part, by the desire to identify homosexuals in the armed forces.

Insurance companies are among those who are especially concerned about identifying people with AIDS or those who might develop it. Since the syndrome leads to devastating illnesses and eventually to death, insurance companies say they need to know whether an applicant is at risk.

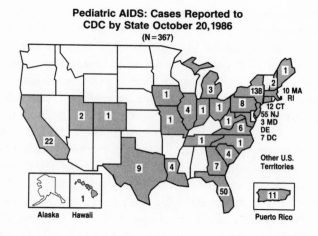

Pediatric AIDS: Cases Reported to CDC by State October 20, 1986
(N = 367)

The National Education Association approved testing of school personnel and students if there is reasonable cause to believe that a person is infected. For example, if the spouse of a person were infected with AIDS, or a school employee has given birth to a child with AIDS, a school may require the individual to submit to a medical evaluation. College administrators have already begun to provide guidelines for dealing with persons who have AIDS, so that steps may be taken to prevent the spread of the syndrome on college campuses without violating civil liberties.

Much controversy about testing in the battle against the spread of AIDS continues. It is important to remember that the detection of antibodies does not mean a person has AIDS or will necessarily develop it. Due to the emotional nature of the subject, if people feel that information about test results will leak out, they may avoid giving blood or becoming involved in anything that demands testing. Some health authorities feel that compulsory testing may work against their own best interests.

Opponents of compulsory testing believe that it will lead to discrimination by employers, landlords, and others. Even though individuals whose tests are positive may not have any symptoms, there are people who fear being near them. In California, Proposition 64 on the November 1986 ballot included a provision making it legal to quarantine and isolate people who are carriers of HIV. This could have resulted in the quarantine of an estimated 300,000 citizens. The proposition was defeated, but it illustrates the kind of thinking that may increase in the future if people are not sensible about dealing with AIDS. Medical information explaining how AIDS is and is not spread has been reported in the media again and again, but irrational fear of AIDS is expected to continue for many years.

Fear of eventually developing full-blown AIDS is realistic for those whose tests indicate they have antibodies to the virus. Their futures are unknown, and many of them say they feel like a walking time bomb. Most of them will probably continue to try to live normal lives, following safe sex guidelines and keeping themselves in good health through proper diet, exercise, and positive thinking. However, people who develop AIDS-related complex can be under even greater stress than those who have full-blown AIDS because of the uncertainty. They may worry about being a burden to others during a long illness and may suffer from depression and fear of death. Even those people who have tested positive for the virus but have no symptoms suffer from some degree of concern, yet this does not mean they cannot function well at their jobs.

While the Justice Department has agreed that AIDS can legally be considered a handicap, it also decreed that the carrier state is not. This opened the way for dismissal of people who carry the antibodies to the AIDS virus even though they show no symptoms of the disease. An employer's concern about the spread of AIDS to other workers or people who came in contact with the person who tested positive could be grounds for dismissal. The ruling was considered irrational by many groups, including the American Medical Association, since casual contact has been ruled out as a means of transmission. This is one wave in a rising tide of legal controversies about AIDS.

While members of many organizations are fighting compulsory testing and discrimination in the workplace, some individuals are asking for tests. Many people who think they have might have been exposed to the AIDS virus at some point in their lives want to go to clinics to find out if they have been infected. Health workers enjoy handing out test results that are negative, but when results are positive, further testing and counseling are available. In some cities, storefront centers offer blood tests and counseling without charge. In 1986, the Centers for Disease Control awarded more than nine million dollars for programs supporting AIDS testing and counseling.

An increasing number of people are in training to counsel people who are concerned about having AIDS as well as those who have been infected. Counseling is often a heartbreaking task. Consider helping a mother with AIDS arrange for the custody of her children. Imagine counseling the pregnant wife of a man with AIDS, knowing that her baby may well be born with the disease. Helping young clients make out their wills is becoming routine even today, and it may become more common in the future. Some counselors say that the most difficult clients to counsel are bisexual men whose wives do not know about their behavior. In clinics and in hospitals, there will be a growing need for health workers to counsel and to provide medical care for people with AIDS.

The first hospital devoted entirely to the care of AIDS patients has already opened its doors in Texas, and numerous hospitals have set up special units for their care. The number of people with AIDS is already straining resources in both cities and suburbs. The future costs of health care for people with AIDS may be staggering.

No one knows how widely the disease will spread in the future, but the battle is being fought on many fronts. Predictions range from bringing the disease under control to an epidemic of catastrophic proportions. Dr. Mathilde Krim, co-chair of the American Foundation for AIDS Research, thinks that recent government reports have not put enough stress on the possibility of greater heterosexual spread. She does note, however, that AIDS should not spread as rapidly in this group as among homosexuals. But almost everyone agrees that the future will bring more cases.

Even in the best of scenarios, AIDS will be with us for years to come. It is an enormous challenge. Surgeon General Koop advises that we would do well to take a look at the future. "We must be prepared to manage those things we can predict, as well as those things we cannot."

AIDS is bound to produce profound changes in our society, and these changes will affect all of us.

Surgeon General's Report on Acquired Immune Deficiency Syndrome

AIDS Caused by Virus

The letters A-I-D-S stand for Acquired Immune Deficiency Syndrome. When a person is sick with AIDS, he/she is in the final stages of a series of health problems caused by a virus (germ) that can be passed from one person to another chiefly during sexual contact or through the sharing of intravenous drug needles and syringes used for "shooting" drugs. Scientists have named the AIDS virus "HIV or HTLV-III or LAV."[1] These abbreviations stand for information denoting a virus that attacks white blood cells (T-Lymphocytes) in the human blood. Throughout this publication, we will call the virus the "AIDS virus." The AIDS virus attacks a person's immune system and damages his/her ability to fight other disease. Without a func-tioning immune system to ward off other germs, he/she now becomes vulnerable to becoming infected by bacteria, protozoa, fungi, and other viruses and malignancies, which may cause life-threatening illness, such as pneumonia, meningitis, and cancer.

No Known Cure
There is presently no cure for AIDS. There is presently no vaccine to prevent AIDS.

Virus Invades Bloodstream
When the AIDS virus enters the bloodstream, it begins to attack certain white blood cells (T-Lymphocytes). Substances called antibodies are produced by the body. These antibodies can be detected in the blood by a simple test, usually two weeks to three months after infection. Even before the antibody test is positive, the victim can pass the virus to others by methods that will be explained.

Once an individual is infected, there are several possibilities. Some people may remain well but even so they are able to infect others. Others may develop a disease that is less serious than AIDS referred to as AIDS Related Complex (ARC). In some people the protective immune system may be destroyed by the virus and then other germs (bacteria, protozoa, fungi, and other

---

[1]These are different names given to AIDS virus by the scientific community.

HIV   — Human immunodeficiency Virus
HTLV-III— Human T-Lymphotropic Virus III
LAV   — Lymphadenopathy Associated Virus

viruses) and cancers that ordinarily would never get a foothold cause "opportunistic diseases . . ." using the *opportunity* of lowered resistance to infect and destroy. Some of the most common are *Pneumocystis carinii* pneumonia and tuberculosis. Individuals infected with the AIDS virus may also develop certain types of cancers such as Kaposi's sarcoma. These infected people have classic AIDS. Evidence shows that the AIDS virus may also attack the nervous system, causing damage to the brain.

SIGNS AND SYMPTOMS
No Signs
Some people remain apparently well after infection with the AIDS virus. They may have no physically apparent symptoms of illness. However, if proper precautions are not used with sexual contacts and/or intravenous drug use, these infected individuals can spread the virus to others. Anyone who thinks he or she is infected or involved in high-risk behaviors should not donate his/her blood, organs, tissues, or sperm because they may now contain the AIDS virus.

ARC
AIDS-Related Complex (ARC) is a condition caused by the AIDS virus in which the patient tests positive for AIDS infection and has a specific set of clinical symptoms. However, ARC patients' symptoms are often less severe than those with the disease we call classic AIDS. Signs and symptoms of ARC may include loss of appetite, weight loss, fever, night sweats, skin rashes, diarrhea, tiredness, lack of resistance to infection, or swollen lymph nodes. These are also signs and symptoms of many other diseases and a physician should be consulted.

AIDS
Only a qualified health professional can diagnose AIDS, which is the result of a natural progress of infection by the AIDS

virus. AIDS destroys the body's immune (defense) system and allows otherwise controllable infections to invade the body and cause additional diseases. These opportunistic diseases would not otherwise gain a foothold in the body. These opportunistic diseases may eventually cause death.

Some symptoms and signs of AIDS and the "opportunistic infections" may include a persistent cough and fever associated with shortness of breath or difficult breathing and maybe the symptoms of *Pneumocystis carinii* pneumonia. Multiple purplish blotches and bumps on the skin may be a sign of Kaposi's sarcoma. The AIDS virus in all infected people is essentially the same; the reactions of individuals may differ.

Long Term
The AIDS virus may also attack the nervous system and cause delayed damage to the brain. This damage may take years to develop and the symptoms may show up as memory loss, indifference, loss of coordination, partial paralysis, or mental disorder. These symptoms may occur alone, or with other symptoms mentioned earlier.

AIDS: THE PRESENT SITUATION
The number of people estimated to be infected with the AIDS virus in the United States is about 1.5 million. All of these individuals are assumed to be capable of spreading the virus sexually (heterosexually or homosexually) or by sharing needles and syringes or other implements for intravenous drug use. Of these, an estimated 100,000 to 200,000 will come down with AIDS-Related Complex (ARC). It is difficult to predict the number who will develop ARC or AIDS because symptoms sometimes take as long as nine years to show up. With our present knowledge, scientists predict that 20 to 30 percent of those infected with the AIDS virus will develop an illness that fits an accepted definition of AIDS within five years. The

number of persons known to have AIDS in the United States to date is over 25,000; of these, about half have died of the disease. Since there is no cure, the others are expected to also eventually die from their disease.

The majority of infected antibody positive individuals who carry the AIDS virus show no disease symptoms and may not come down with the disease for many years, if ever.

No Risk from Casual Contact

There is no known risk of non-sexual infection in most of the situations we encounter in our daily lives. We know that family members living with individuals who have the AIDS virus do not become infected except through sexual contact. There is no evidence of transmission (spread) of AIDS virus by everyday contact even though these family members shared food, towels, cups, razors, even toothbrushes and kissed each other.

Health Workers

We know even more about health-care workers exposed to AIDS patients. About 2,500 health workers who were caring for AIDS patients when they were sickest have been carefully studied and tested for infection with the AIDS virus. These doctors, nurses and other health-care givers have been exposed to the AIDS patients' blood, stool, and other body fluids. Approximately 750 of these health workers reported possible additional exposure by direct contact with a patient's body fluid through spills or being accidentally stuck with a needle. Upon testing these 750, only three who had accidentally stuck themselves with a needle had a positive antibody test for exposure to the AIDS virus. Because health workers had much more contact with patients and their body fluids than would be expected from common everyday contact, it is clear that the AIDS virus is not transmitted by casual contact.

Control of Certain Behaviors Can Stop Further Spread of AIDS

Knowing the facts about AIDS can prevent the spread of the disease. Education of those who risk infecting themselves or infecting other people is the only way we can stop the spread of AIDS. People must be responsible about their sexual behavior and must avoid the use of illicit intravenous drugs and needle sharing. We will describe the types of behavior that lead to infection by the AIDS virus and the personal measures that must be taken for effective protection. If we are to stop the AIDS epidemic, we all must understand the disease—its cause, its nature, and its prevention. *Precautions must be taken.* The AIDS virus infects persons who expose themselves to known risk behavior, such as certain types of homosexual and heterosexual activities or sharing intravenous drug equipment.

Risks

Although the initial discovery was in the homosexual community, AIDS is not a disease only of homosexuals. AIDS is found in heterosexual people as well. AIDS is not a black or white disease. AIDS is not just a male disease. AIDS is found in women; it is found in children. In the future AIDS will probably increase and spread among people who are not homosexual or intravenous drug abusers in the same manner as other sexually transmitted diseases like syphilis and gonorrhea.

Sex Between Men

Men who have sexual relations with other men are especially at risk. About 70 percent of AIDS victims throughout the country are male homosexuals and bisexuals. This percentage probably will decline as heterosexual transmission increases. *Infection results from a sexual relationship with an infected person.*

Multiple Partners

The risk of infection increases according to the number of sexual partners one has, *male or female*. The more partners you have, the greater the risk of becoming infected with the AIDS virus.

How Exposed

Although the AIDS virus is found in several body fluids, a person acquires the virus during sexual contact with an infected person's blood or semen and possibly vaginal secretions. The virus then enters a person's bloodstream through their rectum, vagina, or penis.

Small (unseen by the naked eye) tears in the surface lining of the vagina or rectum may occur during insertion of the penis, fingers, or other objects, thus opening an avenue for entrance of the virus directly into the bloodstream; therefore, the AIDS virus can be passed from penis to rectum and vagina and vice versa without a visible tear in the tissue or the presence of blood.

Prevention of Sexual Transmission—Know Your Partner

Couples who maintain mutually faithful monogamous relationships (only one continuing sexual partner) are protected from AIDS through sexual transmission. If you have been faithful for at least five years and your partner has been faithful too, neither of you is at risk. If you have not been faithful, then you and your partner are at risk. If your partner has not been faithful, then your partner is at risk which also puts you at risk. This is true for both heterosexual and homosexual couples. Unless it is possible to know with *absolute certainty* that neither you nor your sexual partner is not carrying the virus of AIDS, you must use protective behavior. *Absolute certainty* means not only that you and your partner have maintained a mutually faithful monogamous sexual relationship, but it means that neither you nor your partner has used illegal intravenous drugs.

AIDS: YOU CAN PROTECT YOURSELF FROM INFECTION

Some personal measures are adequate to safely protect yourself and others from infection by the AIDS virus and its complications. Among these are:

- If you have been involved in any of the high risk sexual activities described above or have injected illicit intravenous drugs into your body, you should have a blood test to see if you have been infected with the AIDS virus.

- If your test is positive or if you engage in high-risk activities and choose not to have a test, you should tell your sexual partner. If you jointly decide to have sex, you must protect your partner by always using a rubber (condom) during (start to finish) sexual intercourse (vagina or rectum).

- If your partner has a positive blood test showing that he/she has been infected with the AIDS virus or you suspect that he/she has been exposed by previous heterosexual or homosexual behavior or use of intravenous drugs with shared needles and syringes, a rubber (condom) should always be used during (start to finish) sexual intercourse (vagina or rectum).

- If you or your partner is at high risk, avoid mouth contact with the penis, vagina, or rectum.

- Avoid all sexual contact activities which could cause cuts or tears in the linings of the rectum, vagina, or penis.

- Single teenage girls have been warned that pregnancy and contracting sexually transmitted diseases can be the result of only one act of sexual intercourse. They have been taught to say NO to sex! They have been taught to say NO to drugs! By saying NO to sex and drugs, they can avoid AIDS which can kill them! The same is true for teenage boys who should also not have rectal intercourse with other males. It may result in AIDS.

- Do not have sex with prostitutes. Infected male and female prostitutes are frequently also intravenous drug abusers; therefore, they may infect clients by sexual intercourse and other intravenous drug abusers by sharing their intravenous drug equipment. Female prostitutes also can infect their unborn babies.

Intravenous Drug Users

Drug abusers who inject drugs into their veins are another population group at high risk and with high rates of infection by the AIDS virus. Users of intravenous drugs make up 25 percent of the cases of AIDS throughout the country. The AIDS virus is carried in contaminated blood left in the needle, syringe, or other drug-related implements and the virus is injected into the new victim by reusing dirty syringes and needles. Even the smallest amount of infected blood left in a used needle or syringe can contain live AIDS virus to be passed on to the next user of those dirty implements.

No one should shoot up drugs because of addiction, poor health, family disruption, emotional disturbances, and death that follow. However, many drug users are addicted to drugs and for one reason or another have not changed their behavior. For these people, the only way not to get AIDS is *to use a clean, previously unused* needle, syringe, or any other implement necessary for the injection of the drug solution.

Hemophilia

Some persons with hemophilia (a blood clotting disorder that makes them subject to bleeding) have been infected with the AIDS virus either through blood transfusion or the use of blood products that help their blood clot. Now that we know how to prepare safe blood products to aid clotting, this is unlikely to happen. This group represents a very small percentage of the cases of AIDS throughout the country.

Blood Transfusion

Currently all blood donors are initially screened and blood is *not* accepted from high-risk individuals. Blood that has been collected for use is tested for the presence of antibody to the AIDS virus. However, some people may have had a blood transfusion prior to March 1985 before we knew how to screen blood for safe transfusion and may have become infected with the AIDS virus. Fortunately there are not now a large number of these cases. With routine testing of blood products, the blood supply for transfusion is now safer than it has ever been with regard to AIDS.

Persons who have engaged in homosexual activities or have shot street drugs within the last ten years should *never* donate blood.

Mother Can Infect Newborn

If a woman is infected with the AIDS virus and becomes pregnant, she is more likely to develop ARC or classic AIDS, and she can pass the AIDS virus to her unborn child. Approximately one third of the babies born to AIDS-infected mothers will also be infected with the AIDS virus. Most of the infected babies will eventually develop the disease and die. Several of these babies have been born to wives of hemophiliac men infected with the AIDS virus by way of contaminated blood products. Some babies have also been born to women who became infected with the AIDS virus by bisexual partners who had the virus. Almost all babies with AIDS have been born to women who were intravenous drug users or the sexual partners of intravenous drug users who were infected with the AIDS virus. More such babies can be expected.

Think carefully if you plan on becoming pregnant. If there is any chance that you may be in any high-risk group or that you have had sex with someone in a high-risk group, such as homosexual and bisexual males, drug abusers and their sexual partners, see your doctor.

Summary

AIDS affects certain groups of the population. Homosexual and bisexual males who have had sexual contact with other homosexual or bisexual males as well as those who "shoot" street drugs are at greatest risk of exposure, infection and eventual death. Sexual partners of these high risk individuals are at risk, as well as any children born to women who carry the virus. Heterosexual persons are increasingly at risk.

AIDS: WHAT IS SAFE
Most Behavior Is Safe

Everyday living does not present any risk of infection. You *cannot* get AIDS from casual social contact. Casual social contact should not be confused with casual *sexual* contact which is a major cause of the spread of the AIDS virus. Casual *social* contact such as shaking hands, hugging, social kissing, crying, coughing, or sneezing, will not transmit the AIDS virus. Nor has AIDS been contracted from swimming in pools or hot tubs or from eating in restaurants (even if a restaurant worker has AIDS or carries the AIDS virus). AIDS is not contracted from sharing bed linens, towels, cups, straws, dishes, or any other eating utensils. You cannot get AIDS from toilets, doorknobs, telephones, office machinery, or household furniture. You cannot get AIDS from body massages, masturbation, or any non-sexual body contact.

Donating Blood

Donating blood is *not* risky at all. *You cannot get AIDS by donating blood.*

Receiving Blood

In the U.S. every blood donor is screened to exclude high risk persons and every blood donation is now tested for the presence of antibodies to the AIDS virus. Blood that shows exposure to the AIDS virus by the presence of antibodies is not used either for transfusion or for the manufacture of blood products. Blood banks are as safe as current technology can make them. Because antibodies do not form immediately after exposure to the virus, a newly infected person may unknowingly donate blood after becoming infected but before his/her antibody test becomes positive. It is estimated that this might occur less than once in 100,000 transfusions.

There is no danger of AIDS virus infection from visiting a doctor, dentist, hospital, hairdresser, or beautician. AIDS cannot be transmitted nonsexually from an infected person through a health or service provider to another person. Ordinary methods of disinfection for urine, stool, and vomitus which are used for non-infected people are adequate for people who have AIDS or are carrying the AIDS virus. You may have wondered why your dentist wears gloves and perhaps a mask when treating you. This does not mean that he has AIDS or that he thinks you do. He is protecting you and himself from hepatitis, common colds, or flu.

There is no danger in visiting a patient with AIDS or caring for him or her. Normal hygienic practices, like wiping of body fluid spills, with a solution of water and household bleach (1 part household bleach to 10 parts water), will provide full protection.

Children in School

None of the identified cases of AIDS in the United States are known or are suspected to have been transmitted from one child to another in school, day-care, or foster-care settings. Transmission would necessitate exposure of open cuts to the blood or other body fluids of the infected child, a highly unlikely occurrence. Even then routine safety procedures for handling blood or other body fluids (which should be standard for all children in the school or day-care setting) would be effective in preventing transmission from children with AIDS to other children in school.

Children with AIDS are highly susceptible to infections, such as chicken pox, from other children. Each child with AIDS should be examined by a doctor before attending school or before returning to school, day care or foster care settings after an illness. No blanket rules can be made for all schoolboards to cover all possible cases of children with AIDS and each case should be considered separately and individualized to the child and the setting, as would be done with any child with a special problem, such as cerebral palsy or asthma. A good team to make such decisions with the schoolboard would be the child's parents, physician, and a public health official.

Casual social contact between children and persons infected with the AIDS virus is not dangerous.

Insects
There are no known cases of AIDS transmission by insects, such as mosquitoes.

Pets
Dogs, cats, and domestic animals are not a source of infection from AIDS virus.

Tears and Saliva
Although the AIDS virus has been found in tears and saliva, no instance of transmission from these body fluids has been reported.

AIDS comes from sexual contacts with infected persons and from the sharing of syringes and needles. There is no danger of infection with AIDS virus by casual social contact.

Testing of Military Personnel

You may wonder why the Department of Defense is currently testing its uniformed services personnel for presence of AIDS virus antibody. The military feels this procedure is necessary because the uniformed services act as their own blood bank in a time of national emergency. They also need to protect new recruits (who unknowingly may be AIDS virus carriers) from receiving live virus vaccines. These vaccines could activate disease and be potentially life-threatening to the recruits.

AIDS: WHAT IS CURRENTLY UNDERSTOOD

Although AIDS is still a mysterious disease in many ways, our scientists have learned a great deal about it. In five years we know more about AIDS than many diseases that we have studied for even longer periods. While there is no vaccine or cure, the results from the health and behavioral research community can only add to our knowledge and increase our understanding of the disease and ways to prevent and treat it.

In spite of all that is known about transmission of the AIDS virus, scientists will learn more. One possibility is the potential discovery of factors that may better explain the mechanism of AIDS infection.

Why are the antibodies produced by the body to fight the AIDS virus not able to destroy that virus?

The antibodies detected in the blood of carriers of the AIDS virus are ineffective, at least when classic AIDS is actually triggered. They cannot check the damage caused by the virus, which is by then present in large numbers in the body. Researchers cannot explain this important observation. We still do not know why the AIDS virus is not destroyed by man's immune system.

SUMMARY

AIDS no longer is the concern of any one segment of society; it is the concern of us all. No American's life is in danger if he/she or their sexual partners do not engage in high-risk sexual behavior or use shared needles or syringes to inject illicit drugs into the body.

People who engage in high risk sexual behavior or who shoot drugs are risking infection with the AIDS virus and are risking their lives and the lives of others, including their unborn children.

We cannot yet know the full impact of AIDS on our society. From a clinical point of view, there may be new manifestations of AIDS—for example, mental disturbances due to the infection of the brain by the AIDS virus in carriers of the virus. From a social point of view, it may bring to an end the free-wheeling sexual lifestyle which has been called the sexual revolution. Economically, the care of AIDS patients will put a tremendous strain on our already overburdened and costly health care delivery system.

The most certain way to avoid getting the AIDS virus and to control the AIDS epidemic in the United States is for individuals to avoid promiscuous sexual practices, to maintain mutually faithful monogamous sexual relationships and to avoid injecting illicit drugs.

LOOK TO THE FUTURE
The Challenge of the Future

An enormous challenge to public health lies ahead of us and we would do well to take a look at the future. We must be prepared to manage those things we can predict, as well as those we cannot.

At the present time there is no vaccine to prevent AIDS. There is no cure. AIDS, which can be transmitted sexually and by sharing needles and syringes among illicit intravenous drug

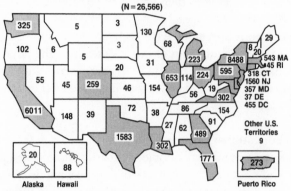

AIDS Cases Reported to CDC by State
United States, Through October 20, 1986
(N = 26,566)

Other U.S. Territories 9

Alaska Hawaii

Puerto Rico

users, is bound to produce profound changes in our society, changes that will affect us all.

Information and Education Only Weapons Against AIDS

It is estimated that in 1991 54,000 people will die from AIDS. At this moment, many of them are not infected with the AIDS virus. With proper information and education, as many as 12,000 to 14,000 people could be saved in 1991 from death by AIDS.

AIDS Will Impact All

The changes in our society will be economic and political and will affect our social institutions, our educational practices, and our health care. Although AIDS may never touch you personally, the societal impact certainly will.

Be Educated—Be Prepared

Be prepared. Learn as much about AIDS as you can. Learn to separate scientific information from rumor and myth. The Public

Health Service, your local public health officials and family physician will be able to help you.

Concern About Spread of AIDS

While the concentration of AIDS cases is in the larger urban areas today, it has been found in every state and with the mobility of our society, it is likely that cases of AIDS will appear far and wide.

Special Educational Concerns

There are a number of people, primarily adolescents, that do not yet know they will be homosexual or become drug users and will not heed this message; there are others who are illiterate and cannot heed this message. They must be reached and taught the risk behaviors that expose them to infection with the AIDS virus.

High Risk Get Blood Test

The greatest public health problem lies in the large number of individuals with a history of high-risk behavior who have been infected with and may be spreading the AIDS virus. Those with high-risk behavior must be encouraged to protect others by adopting safe sexual practices and by the use of clean equipment for intravenous drug use. If a blood test for antibodies to the AIDS virus is necessary to get these individuals to use safe sexual practices, they should get a blood test. Call your local health department for information on where to get the test.

Anger and Guilt

Some people afflicted with AIDS will feel a sense of anger and others a sense of guilt. In spite of these understandable reactions, everyone must join the effort to control the epidemic, to provide for the care of those with AIDS, and to do all we can to inform and educate others about AIDS, and how to prevent it.

Confidentiality

Because of the stigma that has been associated with AIDS, many afflicted with the disease or who are infected with the AIDS virus are reluctant to be identified with AIDS. Because there is no vaccine to prevent AIDS and no cure, many feel there is nothing to be gained by revealing sexual contacts that might also be infected with the AIDS virus. When a community or a state requires reporting of those infected with the AIDS virus to public health authorities in order to trace sexual and intravenous drug contacts—as is the practice with other sexually transmitted diseases—those infected with the AIDS virus have gone underground out of the mainstream of health care and education. For this reason current public health practice is to protect the privacy of the individual infected with the AIDS virus and to maintain the strictest confidentiality concerning his/her health records.

State and Local AIDS Task Forces

Many state and local jurisdictions where AIDS has been seen in the greatest numbers have AIDS task forces with heavy representation from the field of public health joined by others who can speak broadly to issues of access to care, provision of care and the availability of community and psychiatric support services. Such a task force is needed in every community with the power to develop plans and policies, to speak, and to act for the good of the public health at every level.

State and local task forces should plan ahead and work collaboratively with other jurisdictions to reduce transmission of AIDS by far-reaching informational and educational programs. As AIDS impacts more strongly on society, they should be charged with making recommendations to provide for the needs of those afflicted with AIDS. They also will be in the best position to answer the concerns and direct the activities of those who are not infected with the AIDS virus.

The responsibility of state and local task forces should be far reaching and might include the following areas:

- Insure enforcement of public health regulation of such practices as ear piercing and tattooing to prevent transmission of AIDS virus.
- Conduct AIDS education programs for police, fireman, correctional institution workers, and emergency medical personnel for dealing with AIDS victims and the public.
- Insure that institutions catering to children or adults who soil themselves or their surroundings with urine, stool, and vomitus have adequate equipment for cleanup and disposal, and have policies to insure the practice of good hygiene.

School

Schools will have special problems in the future. In addition to the guidelines already mentioned in this pamphlet, there are other things that should be considered such as sex education and education of the handicapped.

Sex Education

Education concerning AIDS must start at the lowest grade possible as part of any health and hygiene program. The appearance of AIDS could bring together diverse groups of parents and educators with opposing views on inclusion of sex education in the curricula. There is now no doubt that we need sex education in schools and that it include information on heterosexual and homosexual relationships. The threat of AIDS should be sufficient to permit a sex education curriculum with a heavy emphasis on prevention of AIDS and other sexually transmitted diseases.

Handicapped and Special Education

Children with AIDS or ARC will be attending school along with others who carry the AIDS virus. Some children will develop brain disease which will produce changes in mental behavior. Because of the right to special education of the handicapped and the mentally retarded, schoolboards and higher authorities will have to provide guidelines for the management of such children on a case-by-case basis.

Labor and Management

Labor and management can do much to prepare for AIDS so that misinformation is kept to a minimum. Unions should issue preventive health messages because many employees will listen more carefully to a union message than they will to one from public health authorities.

AIDS Education at the Work Site

Offices, factories, and other work sites should have a plan in operation for education of the work force and accommodation of AIDS or ARC patients before the first such case appears at the work site. Employees with AIDS or ARC should be dealt with as are any workers with a chronic illness. In-house video programs provide an excellent source of education and can be individualized to the needs of a specific work group.

Strain on the Health Care Delivery System

The health care system in many places will be overburdened as it is now in urban areas with large numbers of AIDS patients. It is predicted that during 1991 there will be 145,000 patients requiring hospitalization at least once and 54,000 patients who will die of AIDS. Mental disease (dementia) will occur in some patients who have the AIDS virus before they have any other manifestation such as ARC or classic AIDS.

State and local task forces will have to plan for these patients by utilizing conventional and time honored systems but will also have to investigate alternate methods of treatment and alternate sites for care including homecare.

The strain on the health system can be lessened by family, social, and psychological support mechanisms in the community. Programs are needed to train chaplains, clergy, social workers, and volunteers to deal with AIDS. Such support is critical to the minority communities.

Mental Health
Our society will also face an additional burden as we better understand the mental health implications of infection by the AIDS virus. Upon being informed of infection with the AIDS virus, a young, active, vigorous person faces anxiety and depression brought on by fears associated with social isolation, illness, and dying. Dealing with these individual and family concerns will require the best efforts of mental health professionals.

Controversial Issues
A number of controversial AIDS issues have arisen and will continue to be debated largely because of lack of knowledge about AIDS, how it is spread, and how it can be prevented. Among these are the issues of compulsory blood testing, quarantine, and identification of AIDS carriers by some visible sign.

Compulsory Blood Testing
Compulsory blood testing of individuals is not necessary. The procedure could be unmanageable and cost prohibitive. It can be expected that many who *test* negatively might actually be positive due to *recent* exposure to the AIDS virus and give a false sense of security to the individual and his/her sexual partners concerning necessary protective behavior. The prevention behavior described in this report, if adopted, will protect the American public and contain the AIDS epidemic. Voluntary testing will be available to those who have been involved in high risk behavior.

Quarantine

Quarantine has no role in the management of AIDS because AIDS is not spread by casual contact. The only time that some form of quarantine might be indicated is in a situation where an individual carrying the AIDS virus knowingly and willingly continues to expose others through sexual contact or sharing drug equipment. Such circumstances should be managed on a case-by-case basis by local authorities.

Identification of AIDS Carriers by Some Visible Sign

Those who suggest the marking of carriers of the AIDS virus by some visible sign have not thought the matter through thoroughly. It would require testing of the entire population which is unnecessary, unmanageable, and costly. It would miss those recently infected individuals who would test negatively, but be infected. The entire procedure would give a false sense of security. AIDS must and will be treated as a disease that can infect anyone. AIDS should not be used as an excuse to discriminate against any group or individual.

Updating Information

As the Surgeon General, I will continually monitor the most current and accurate health, medical, and scientific information and make it available to you, the American people. Armed with this information you can join in the discussion and resolution of AIDS-related issues that are critical to your health, your children's health, and the health of the nation.

Groups Offering AIDS Information and Support

Centers for Disease Control
Hot line: 1-800-342-AIDS
1-800-443-0366
(In Atlanta: (404) 329-3534)

National Institute of Allergy
and Infectious Diseases
Office of Research Reporting
and Public Response
(301)496-5717

Public Health Service
Hot line (general information): 1-800-342-2437
Hot line (specific questions):
1-800-447-AIDS

AIDS Action Council
Federation of AIDS-Related
Organizations
729 8th St, SE
Suite 200
Washington, DC 20003
(202) 547-3101

American Association of
Physicians for Human
Rights
PO Box 14366
San Francisco, CA 94114
(415) 558-9353

Fund for Human Dignity
666 Broadway
New York, NY 10012
(212) 529-1600
1-800-221-7044

Lambda Legal Defense and
  Education Fund
666 Broadway
New York, NY 10012
(212) 995-8585

National AIDS Network
729 8th St, SE
Suite 300
Washington, DC 20003
(202) 546-2424

National Gay and Lesbian
  Task Force
1517 U St, NW
Washington, DC 20009
1-800-221-7044 or (202) 332-
  6483

National Hemophilia Foundation
Soho Building
110 Greene St, Room 406
New York, NY 10012
(212) 219-8180

National Lesbian and Gay
  Health Foundation
PO Box 65472
Washington, DC 20035
(202) 797-3708

Glossary

Acquired Immune Deficiency Syndrome: See AIDS

Active immunity: Protection against a disease resulting from the production of antibodies in a person or animal that has been inoculated with an antigen. (Compare with passive immunity.)

AIDS: A disease caused by HIV (human immunodeficiency virus) that is characterized by a deficiency in the immune system and the development of certain diseases. The virus attacks the brain in some patients even before they show symptoms of the diseases commonly found among people with AIDS.

AIDS-related complex (ARC): A variety of chronic symptoms and physical findings that appear related to AIDS but do not meet the Centers for Disease Control definition. The immune system may be less severely damaged than in AIDS. ARC may or may not progress to AIDS. ARC can be fatal.

Antibody: A blood protein produced by mammals in response to exposure to a specific antigen. Antibodies are a critical component of the immune system.

Antigen: A large molecule which, when introduced into the body, stimulates the production of an antibody that will react specifically with that antigen.

Autologous transfusion: A blood transfusion in which the patient receives his or her own blood, donated several weeks before surgery.

B-lymphocytes (B-cells): Lymphocytes that mediate immune reactions. B-lymphocytes proliferate under stimulation from factors released by T-lymphocytes.

Candida albicans: A yeast-like fungus commonly found in the mucous membranes of the mouth, intestines, and vagina, capable of causing a variety of infections such as thrush.

Clone: A group of genetically identical cells or an organism produced asexually from a common ancestor.

Cofactor: A factor other than the basic causative agent of a disease that increases the likelihood of developing the disease.

Cytomegalovirus (CMV): Any of a group of herpes viruses. Although it rarely causes disease in healthy adults, it may produce pneumonia, inflammation of the retina, liver, kidneys, and colon in people with AIDS.

DNA (deoxyribonucleic acid): A linear polymer that is the carrier of genetic information in living organisms. Recombinant DNA is a hybrid DNA formed by joining pieces of DNA from different organisms in vitro.

ELISA: An acronym for enzyme-linked immunosorbent assay. A test used to detect antibodies against HIV in blood samples.

Encephalitis: Inflammation of the brain.

Enzyme: Any group of proteins produced by living cells that mediate and promote the chemical processes of life without themselves being altered or destroyed.

Epidemiologic studies: Studies concerned with the relationships of various factors determining the frequency and distribution of specific diseases in a human community.

Epstein-Barr virus: One of the herpes viruses believed to cause infectious mononucleosis and Burkitt's lymphoma.

Factor VIII: A naturally occurring protein in plasma that aids in the coagulation of blood. A congenital deficiency of Factor VIII results in the bleeding disorder known as hemophilia A.

Gene: The basic unit of heredity; an ordered sequence of nucleotide bases, comprising a segment of DNA.

Gene expression: The mechanisms through which directions contained within the genes that code for a cell's products are transferred and used to direct the production process.

Hemophilia: A rare, hereditary bleeding disorder caused by a deficiency in the ability to synthesize one or more of the proteins involved in coagulating the blood.

Hepatitis: Inflammation of the liver; may be due to many causes, including viruses, several of which are transmissible through blood transfusions.

Herpes simplex: An acute disease caused by herpes simplex viruses types 1 and 2. Groups of watery blisters, often painful, form on the skin and mucous membranes, especially the borders of the lips (cold sores) or the mucous surface of the genitals.

Herpesvirus group: A group of viruses that includes the herpes simplex viruses, the varicella-zoster virus (the cause of chicken pox and shingles), cytomegalovirus, and Epstein-Barr virus.

HIV (human immunodeficiency virus): The name proposed for the causative agent of AIDS by a subcommittee of the International Committee on the Taxonomy of Viruses. (*See* HTLV-III, and LAV.)

HTLV-III (human T-cell lymphotropic virus, type III): A newly discovered retrovirus that is believed to be the basic cause of AIDS. The target organ of HTLV-III is the T-4 subset of T-lymphocytes, which are the master regulators of the immune system.

Immune: Being highly resistant to a disease because of the formation of humoral antibodies or the development of cellular immunity, or both, or as a result of some other mechanism such as interferon activity in viral infections.

Interferon: A class of glycoproteins (proteins with carbohydrates attached at specific locations) important in immune function and thought to inhibit viral infections.

In vitro: Literally, "in glass"; often used in reference to the growth of cells from multicellular organisms under cell culture conditions.

In vivo: Literally, "in the living"; pertaining to a biological reaction taking place in a living organism.

Kaposi's sarcoma: A multifocal, spreading cancer of the connective tissue, principally involving the skin; it usually begins on the toes or the feet as reddish blue or brownish soft nodules and tumors.

LAV (lymphodenopathy-association virus): A retrovirus recovered from a person with lymphodenopathy (enlarged lymph glands) and also in a group at high risk for AIDS, and now believed to be the same virus as HTLV-III.

Lymphocytes: Specialized white blood cells involved in the immune response.

Mutation: A change in the genetic material of a virus or a cell that may lead to a change in the structure of function of a protein.

Opportunistic infection: A disease or infection caused by a microorganism that does not ordinarily cause disease but which, under certain circumstances such as impaired immune responses, becomes pathologic.

Passive immunity: Disease resistance in a person or animal due to the injection of antibodies from another person or animal. Passive immunity is usually short lasting.

Pneumocystis carinii pneumonia: A type of pneumonia primarily found in infants and now commonly occurring in patients with AIDS.

Retrovirus: A virus that contains RNA, not DNA, and that produces a DNA analog of its RNA through the production of an enzyme known as "reverse transcriptase." The resulting DNA is incorporated in the genetic structure of the invaded cell in a form referred to as "pro-virus."

Reverse transcriptase: An enzyme produced by retroviruses that allows them to produce a DNA copy of their RNA.

RNA (ribonucleic acid): Any of various nucleic acids that contain ribose and uracil as structural components and are associated with the control of cellular chemical activities.

Seropositive: A condition in which antibodies to a particular disease-producing organism are found in the blood.

Serum: The clear portion of any animal liquid separated from its more solid elements, especially the clear liquid (blood serum) that separates in the clotting of blood.

Syndrome: A pattern of symptoms that together characterize a particular disease or disorder.

T-cell growth factor (also known as interleukin-2): A glycoprotein that is released by T-lymphocytes on stimulation with antigens and functions as a T-cell growth factor by inducing proliferation of activated T-cells.

T-lymphocytes (T-cells): Lymphocytes that mature in the thymus and that mediate cellular immune reactions. T-lymphocytes also release factors that induce proliferation of T-lymphocytes and B-lymphocytes.

Vaccine: A preparation of killed organisms, living attenuated organisms, living fully virulent organisms, or parts of microorganisms, that is administered to produce or artificially increase immunity to a particular disease.

Virus: Any of a large group of submicroscopic agents capable of infecting plants, animals, and bacteria, and characterized by a total dependence on living cells for reproduction and by a lack of independent metabolism.

Western Blot Technique: A test believed to be more specific than the ELISA in detecting antibodies in blood samples.

Index

THE AUTHORS

Margaret O. Hyde, a resident of Shelburne, Vermont, is the author of more than fifty books for young people and several documentaries for NBC-TV. In addition to writing and teaching, she has served as science consultant for the Lincoln School of Teachers College, Columbia University.

Elizabeth H. Forsyth, a psychiatrist, has collaborated with Margaret O. Hyde on three previous books. A graduate of the Yale University School of Medicine, she has served as clinical instructor in psychiatry at University of Vermont College of Medicine, has been psychiatric consultant for the Burlington, Vermont, public school system, and currently combines private practice with forensic psychiatry.

Hyde and Forsyth have collaborated on a number of significant titles including: *Know Your Feelings, What Have You Been Eating?, Suicide: The Hidden Epidemic,* and *Terrorism: A Special Kind of Violence.*